Brinnovation User Testin

D1110283

"I recently joined a company where a new te~ ~..~gy platform was being developed for over a year. Two months after joining the company, I developed a new technology platform in three days using your methodology." —**An IT Development Engineer**

"The methodology helps in identifying all the dependencies involved and all the things to consider in completing the innovative solution faster. It will reduce the time to innovate by at least 40–60 percent. If you go through the process, you know more about what you don't know, which otherwise would be realized much later. The methodology identifies weak areas of the innovation cycle for prioritization or allocating resources. Sometimes people have fears of failure or preconceived notions that the solution will not work. The methodology systematically encourages experimentation and alleviates fears of failure. The methodology motivates goal-driven thinking or aspirations for innovation (the absence of which is the first barrier to innovation)." —**A Product Development Engineer at a Telecom Company**

"[I] taught innovation and entrepreneurship along with Praveen Gupta at Illinois Institute of Technology (IIT). We have recognized distinct roles of innovation and entrepreneurship for the success of a business. His methods and tools plant and nourish seeds of innovation that his students will utilize for a long time after completing their education. *The Innovation Solution* book offers excellent framework and tools to sustain innovation in any organization for continual success." —**C. Robert Carlson, Dean, School of Applied Technology, Illinois Institute of Technology**

More Praise for *The Innovation Solution...*

"This is a *must read* for anybody interested in innovation. In a compact, easy-to-follow style, the book offers the best innovation strategies, methodologies, and tools, including how to change the culture to make innovation a pervasive daily business. This will ensure your organization's sustainable growth and agility." —**Adina Suciu, MBNQA Award Examiner and Consultant, Seattle, WA**

"Intense global competition demands that companies of all sizes need to innovate at all levels including new products and services as part of the everyday business process. Gupta's *Innovation Solution* provides a framework of innovation on demand any company can use to survive and thrive in today's ever-changing marketplace." **—Jim Correll, Facilitator/Business Coach, Independence Community College, Independence, KS**

"*The Innovation Solution* book is a concise description of innovation. The introduction of the TEDOC provides a useful model to develop any new product or service. A useful reference for anyone trying to innovate!" **—John Forsberg, Certified Master Business Innovator, Trainer and Consultant, Schaumburg, IL**

"*The Innovation Solution*, is a highly practical book for anyone interested in better understanding and applying the tenets of innovation to help drive their companies to greater levels of performance and profitability. A must read for anyone who intends to succeed in the 21st century!" **—Peter G. Balbus, Managing Director, Pragmaxis, LLC**

"*The Innovation Solution* book provides the context, framework, tools, and operating guidelines to actually make innovation happen from grassroots level to a commercially viable business." **—Atulya Nath, CEO, Global Institute of Intellectual Property, New Delhi, India**

"Praveen's innovation framework is a great way to teach innovation at universities around the world because he expands basic elements of innovation to the most complete knowledge. One can use his methods immediately." **—Rubén Pablo García, Ortegón International Relationships, Universidad Technological of León, León Guanajuato, México**

"*The Innovation Solution* simplifies knowledge of innovation and presents concepts and methods to innovate on demand." **—Jorge Oliveira Teixeira, MBA, Managing Partner of Accelper Consulting Iberia, Portugal**

"Creativity and business innovation can be learned. *The Innovation Solution* provides the framework to learn and tools to achieve reliable, innovative results that businesses require for sustaining profitable growth." **—Ed Coates, Certified Master Business Innovator, Faculty, Lebanon Valley College, Annville, PA**

The Innovation Solution

Making Innovation More Pervasive,
Predictable and Profitable

Praveen Gupta

Other books by Praveen Gupta

Business Innovation in the 21st Century

———

Six Sigma Business Scorecard

———

The Six Sigma Performance Handbook

———

The Complete and Balanced Service Scorecard

———

Improving Healthcare Quality and Cost with Six Sigma

———

First Edition 2011

Gupta, Praveen

The Innovation Solution

Published by Accelper Consulting/ CreateSpace, an Amazon.com Company

To obtain permission to translate this book into other languages, to buy from stock, or to receive a bulk quantity discount, please contact Accelper Consulting at:

e-mail: info@accelper.com

Fax: (847) 884-7280

Tel: (847) 884-1900

ISBN: 1456558102

ISBN 13: 9781456558109

Dedicated to

All my teachers

Contents

Foreword

I first met Praveen in 2009. He was the keynote speaker and presented a highly spirited message on innovation to the Chicago Technology Executive Network in Chicago. I immediately recognized that morning he was touching on a subject that was immensely important to every leader in that room. He was challenging each one of us with the question of whether we would have the courage and even the audacity to take the lead in creating an *innovative* spirit throughout our organizations.

That day, Praveen spoke to the heart of most organization's core issue for thriving in a highly competitive market—that is, being less focused on cost-cutting and streamlining, and more invested and committed to building a culture of innovation. In his most recent book, *The Innovation Solution*, he builds the case that like most things, *innovation* can be learned, and when every individual in the organization is learning and practicing innovation, dramatic and significant results occur.

Based on Praveen's inspiration, I spearheaded an Innovation Day for my company and invited all our employees to hear how innovation was occurring in our organization. It was an opportunity for them to hear the insightful messages delivered by Praveen and other well-known authors of innovation. Along with the inspirational messages on innovation, his most recent book was provided to our employees to help them further understand the innovation process and inspire new thinking and approaches in the workplace.

This book provides those who have the desire to create an innovative environment in their organization the process and instructions to fuel innovation and growth. I sincerely believe Praveen is ahead of his time in developing a systematic approach to teaching innovation, and it would be my belief that in the next five years, we will see universities and institutions of higher learning teaching innovation processes as part of their standard curriculum. I highly recommend this book for those who view innovation as the key to the success and bright future of their organizations.

William Bradford
Global Director of Operations

Preface

Since developing the breakthrough innovation framework in 2005, my colleagues and I have come a long way. We introduced the framework on online bulletin boards for quick feedback and then at professional meetings for personal reactions. Finally, we presented it in articles to be shared with larger audiences and received their feedback. The feedback was always positive and exciting. This enthusiasm led us to publish a very comprehensive book on innovation titled *Business Innovation in the 21st Century*. This book included contributions from industry experts along with the framework for breakthrough innovation.

The breakthrough innovation framework became the basis for a college-level business innovation course that has enjoyed over five years of enrollment. Students are learning the business innovation framework, enjoying the class, and applying the concepts at their workplaces. Some of them have sent thank-you notes along with their success stories. For example, one practitioner said that what he developed over a weekend would have taken him more than six months on his own. Another student said that his company had tried to develop a new technology platform for over one and a half years, and he developed one in three days using the breakthrough innovation methodology.

Business Innovation in the 21st Century has already been published in Portuguese, and it is currently being translated into Spanish. Additionally, the book has been published in India for the Southeast Asian market by the S. Chand Group.

After offering the business innovation class for six semesters, I launched a training and certification program in collaboration with the Illinois Institute of Technology. The intent of the training and certification program is to provide the training to busy professionals in a shorter time frame and enable them to develop innovative solutions faster.

In addition to the book and the training program, the *International Journal of Innovation Science* was also launched by Accelper Consulting in conjunction with Multi-Science Publishing in the United Kingdom. The intent of the journal is to promote the science of innovation for professional use in a repeatable manner. The first Business Innovation Conference was held in September 2008 and provided an opportunity to exchange ideas in the field of business innovation. With all these initiatives in place, a task force to develop innovation standards will be assembled very shortly.

While the various pieces to promote business innovation finally started to come together, there still appeared to be a need for a book that offered a simple innovation solution for everyone to jump-start the process. I wrote *The Innovation Solution* to accomplish that objective.

Fortunately, I have enjoyed my innovation journey with many friends, students, colleagues, and mentors since 2005. While I know I will miss some names, I do want to acknowledge Paul Davis, Natasha Tong, Suresh Shenoy, Abhai Johri, Venkat Ravilla, Nickhil Mahabaleshwar, Mohit Gaonkar, Adam Hartung, Peter Balbus, Phil McEntee, Gurinder Singh, Ray Mehra, Tarun Kumar, Nand Prakash Garg, Pradeep Goel, Steve DuBrow, Carl Vizza, Janet Reif, Ruth Sweester, Nik Rokop, Brett Trusko, Heather Van Sickle, Scott Pfeiffer, Dan Brown, Veer Khare, Divya Chekki, Rajiv Khanna, Nichole Novak, John Forsberg, Siri Chakka, William Bradford, Aditya Nath, William Wentz, and Robert Carlson. I would like to extend special thanks to my friends at Microsoft, especially Adam Hecktman and Krishna Kumar, for sharing their expertise and sponsoring the Student Innovator Award for my business innovation class.

I would also like to express my gratitude to my international friends Alberto Casal, Irena Suznjevic, Slavko Vidović, Luís Filipe Reis, João Mendes, Jorge Teixeira, and many more for their enthusiastic support and partnerships. Special thanks go to Miguel Peixoto de Sousa and João Luis Sousa of Vida Economica for publishing *Business Innovation in the 21st Century* in Portuguese and Dinesh Jhunjhunwala and Nirmala Gupta of S. Chand & Group for publishing the book for the Indian Subcontinent.

I extend personal gratitude to Arvind Srivastava, Dan Pongetti, and Shellie Tate for their unwavering commitment to publishing this book, and the PANIIT2009 Global Conference team for distributing a copy of the its pre-publication edition to about two thousand attendees.

Enjoy innovating!

Praveen Gupta
May 1, 2011

The Innovation Express

A word to professionals traveling the innovation journey:

The journey in innovation is much easier when you have a guide and a coach like Praveen Gupta along for the ride. *The Innovation Solution* brings you, the practitioner, an express solution to transitioning from the traditional to the innovative way of getting around, which is vital in the very competitive global marketplace. Innovation without the passion to succeed, however, is like a jet aircraft without the jet fuel. Armed with the techniques for innovation and your passion for finding solutions, anything is possible. Knowing Praveen for over a decade as a professional has been both a pleasure and an honor. He approaches everything in life with passion and gusto. To get the most out of *The Innovation Solution*, you must commit yourself to the processes and principles presented herein. I send my very best wishes for a very pleasant journey to Praveen and the riders on the Innovation Express.

Ray Mehra
CEO, R-Squared

Chapter One

The Innovation Dilemma

Innovation has been a topic of discussion for over twenty-five years. In 1985, Peter Drucker published the seminal article on this subject, entitled "The Discipline of Innovation," followed by a book, *Innovation and Entrepreneurship*, which led us in the direction of thinking in terms of the innovation process. Also around that time, Robert W. Weisberg, the author of "Creativity, Genius and other Myths" published in 1986 said the time was right for somebody to develop a theory of creativity. Concurrently, the world's largest economy—the United States—started experiencing serious global competition.

While the American companies' focus for achieving growth could have been on innovation, the key approach employed to achieve their profit objectives became cost reduction—the path of least resistance. An operational excellence approach took over innovation. While cost reduction accelerated with the use of tools like Six Sigma and Lean, innovation was incubating. Making a profit is not a bad goal; the issue is whether that should be the *only* objective. What about sustaining profit growth over a period of time by developing new products, services, and solutions that the customer will value?

Tools to achieve the profit objective did have some short-term positive impact on the companies' bottom lines; however, their sustainability was questionable in the absence of a strategy for growth through business innovation. The continual slimming of processes leads to corporate anorexia, and use of Lean and Six Sigma like methodologies for reducing waste of resources may lead to analysis paralysis. For over two decades, the main measures of continual improvement have been cost reduction and profit. Unfortunately, businesses always run out of savings if they use Lean and Six Sigma without adopting innovation to exploit growth opportunities.

While the corporate world was busy with cost reduction, governments and business schools were busy working on making laws, policies, and strategies that promoted innovation. These organizations focused extensively on measuring innovation impact specifically. For example, a CEO at a major corporation, inspired by what he had seen in current work on innovation, asked his team to read an innovation book and let him know if they needed any help or if he should summon an innovation expert. Sadly, no one from his staff called him to talk about innovation. In spite of IBM studying global trends, McKinsey doing a variety of surveys, experts writing an unlimited number of books, consultants selling numerous methodologies, and thought leaders giving inspirational talks using examples from the eighties, people remain confused—skeptics at best—and progress has been very inefficient and limited at best. We need to do better.

As executives, we understand that innovation is one of our top three priorities. However, we do not really know how to strategize, where to start, which resources we need, or what to expect. We wonder how to wrap our heads around this "buzz" concept of innovation as we read conflicting stories authored by great consulting companies in leading business magazines. As a result of these complications, innovation actually lost some of its popularity and glamour, but it is still the talk of practically every meeting. The dilemma is we want to do it, but we do not understand innovation well enough to lead it in our companies.

This is true for everyone! We are all born to be creative, just like we are all born with the instinct to walk. We are all creative; this is how we as humans figured out how to survive for such a long time. The challenge at present lies in learning to meet the objective to win the race in the presence of global competition. To run a race, one must train. Let's think about our posture as we walk and run. Which body part leads the race? We all walk and run with our feet, but we race with our heads. In most races, we face intense competition and require speed to win. Just like training is required to win races, people need training to succeed in the innovation race.

Sometimes, we feel helpless and clueless. In the absence of clear guidance, we don't even know what innovation means anymore. The good news is that we are not alone. Even the definition of *innovation* is evolving. Innovation is not just about creating a novel solution; instead, for a business, it now implies creating something unique that customers enjoy, can benefit from immensely, or for which they are willing to pay. The following is a practical definition of innovation for businesses:

Innovation is continually and efficiently developing and delivering breakthrough solutions by offering higher value to customers, achieving profitable growth for businesses, and gaining competitive advantages in the marketplace.

Who in an organization should lead the innovation? In the information age, new value needs to be created continually for the exploding volume of information. In addition, innovation is no longer limited to products or services. It must be in every aspect of business; it is the cumulative advantage of all the innovations in an organization that provides a great competitive advantage. For example, iPod is not simply a product innovation; instead, iPod is a system comprised of many innovations in applications, products, distribution, personalization, branding, sales, service, supply chain, and accessories.

We cannot simply think of innovating something and trying to sell it; instead, we must set our minds to innovate systems that provide an enjoyable experience for customers if we want a large number of people to pay for it. In order for us to accomplish such a level of innovation and obtain its associated competitive advantage, innovation must be institutionalized and must leverage the capabilities of all employees. Such a broad deployment of innovation requires information, technology and people. The IT department deals with information and technology to affect people. It is no coincidence that when I tried to introduce my business innovation course through a business school or industrial engineering program, I ended up teaching the innovation course in the Information Technology Management department. When other departments recognized the need for innovation, the students from these departments were allowed to attend this business innovation class.

Information leads to analytics, analytics leads to intelligence, and intelligence leads to knowledge that creates a driving hunger for more new knowledge and innovation. And this creates an excellent opportunity for IT folks to turn their value proposition from justifying their existence as cost-centers to generating innovative solutions for business growth. The executive title of chief information officer evolves into chief innovation officer.

The Fundamental Business Strategy

In a growing economy, we are less risk averse and are willing to justify waste in the name of creating new opportunity. In a shrinking economy, however, we shift our focus to cutting costs, reducing waste, and staying afloat or maybe profitable. Such a state of business management pits profit against growth, cost-cutting against investment, excellence against innovation, and job reduction against job creation.

In order to manage the bottom line and the top line independently, we need to think in a totally different way. Our strategies are distinct and appear to be in contention. For example, if a company is focusing on cutting cost, the outcome is a set of activities to cut cost. This suicidal approach to business launches the business on a downward spiral that eventually leads to demise. A company can pursue profitable growth, but it requires a lot of thinking. To explore growth opportunities, innovation is necessary. Growth creates hope and excitement, while pursuing cost management alone leads to fear and stress.

Mergers and acquisitions (M&A) have been a norm for achieving revenue growth. Mergers and Acquisitions Global Research Report by KPMG published in 1999 discovered the success rate of M&As in achieving their intended objectives at 17 percent. Many successful companies develop a combination of M&A-driven and organic growth. Both of these approaches have led to some successes, but not like the executives would love to have seen. In a global economy, the shrinking product lifecycle's dependency on organic growth increasingly requires an innovation process that is agile, effective, efficient, and manageable. Pursuing such an innovation strategy, however, requires us to come to terms with the following:

1. Evolving definitions of innovation

2. The effectiveness of innovation

3. The efficiency of innovation

4. The extent of innovation

5. The return on innovation

6. The rate of innovation

7. Numerous methodologies

8. Measures of Innovation

Venture-funded projects have an expected success rate of about 10 percent; R&D-driven innovation has a success rate of 5 to 10 percent, and M&As, as mentioned, have a success rate of about 17 percent. In other words, everything that is required to contribute to traditional business growth has a very low success rate. At the same time, we keep pushing manufacturing and operations to the success rate of almost 100 percent. There is a disproportionate emphasis on excellence in operations and other aspects of business.

In reality, businesses have been failing in spite of applying Lean or Six Sigma methodologies. Factors other than operations have a significant impact on corporate performance. Our research shows that operations impact only about 10 percent of the corporate performance, implying that other areas are even more significant to the success of a corporation. Figure 1.1 shows a breakdown of the significance of corporate performance elements:

BUSINESS PROCESS / FUNCTION	SIGNIFICANCE	ROLE
Leadership (CEO & Staff)	30%	Inspire & Reward
Management	20%	Accelerate Improvement
Employee Involvement	10%	Innovate Solutions
Sales and Distribution	10%	Revenue Growth
Purchasing & Supply Chain	10%	Quality & Cost
Operations Excellence	10%	Optimization & Excellence
Customer Service & Growth	10%	Trends & Delight
Total	**100%**	

FIGURE 1.1 Elements of Corporate Performance

The CEO and leadership staff's decisions carry a huge weight in corporate success. Middle management has an equally significant role in striving for perfection, and their focus must be on leading improvement rather than managing people. In knowledge age, people normally do not need a lot of supervision. Once leaders and managers develop the right framework—the balancing of revenue versus cost and optimization versus investment—innovation can easily be managed.

The Innovation Dilemma

Executives are willing to invest in innovation, research, development, and employee idea management. They get frustrated at not getting enough financial returns fast enough or even worse, when innovations cause losses. Many products report losses during their early years when companies use the conventional new product development (NPD) processes. The conventional NPD processes are more a cautious approach to managing the uncertainty and risks associated with the product development than a contribution to innovation.

These NPD processes do not really encourage innovation. I have seen companies launch new products by simply tightening design tolerances, thinking the customer will thus get improved performance, but the customer sees no benefit. In reality, such innovations cause manufacturing nightmares, adding fuel to the fire instead of putting it out, and perpetuate adverse trends in profitable growth.

Executives want to invest in innovation, but in this day and age, there is no assurance or guarantee of results. So we spend more time identifying risks than creating rewards for successes. Corporations and academic institutions investing in research on innovation methods need to collaborate and take the lead in providing this assurance, instead of teaching entrepreneurship for managing innovations that we do not know much about.

Creativity is a prerequisite for innovation, because innovation is applied creativity. Entrepreneurship is about monetizing innovation. Excellence in execution is a prerequisite for successful entrepreneurship. There is no shortage of academic programs on entrepreneurship; however, there are limited options for learning about innovation.

One of the main reasons for executive frustration with innovation is that the time needed to see returns on innovation using current innovation processes is about five to seven years. The information age, however, has accelerated reduction in the product life cycle from a few years to a few months; hence, we find a significant mismatch at a very fundamental level. Research shows that conventional methods used for developing new products—even at innovative companies—have a return on investment of about $0.17 annually. On the other hand, knowledge-economy companies have a return on investment of about $0.80 annually. The recovery of investment in this new economy using the conventional innovation methods can take forever. Therefore, the innovation process must be taught, mastered, and accelerated throughout the organization. Innovation should no longer be considered the result of a flash of genius; instead, it should be targeted to making everyone a genius.

Even Albert Einstein was known as Albert in his early days. He was not the best student in his class. However, he must have been curious and reflective about what he was seeing in his dad's factory or what he was learning about. His contribution changed significantly soon after he started working in the trademarks and patents office in Zurich in 1902. Interestingly, all four of his papers were published in 1905. What changed? When one works in a trademarks and patents office, one gets to learn about other people's creative work, thus generating one's own new ideas.

Luckily for us, being innovative today does not require working at a patent and trademark office; anyone with a strong desire can realize innovation. Everyone has access to trademark and patent offices and can learn what others are doing, what the areas of discovery are, and how to identify new opportunities for innovation. In other words, companies must mine a database of trademarks and patents to tune into the earliest discoveries.

Interestingly, most of the Einstein's work was in his mind, and he conducted numerous thought experiments. Einstein had multiple major discoveries about the fundamentals of the universe, received a few patents and won a Nobel Prize. At the other side of the spectrum, Thomas Edison was a hands-on innovator. He mastered the process of inventing and innovating and received many patents (over a thousand). He believed he could innovate anytime and planned to have a patent a week. He must have believed in the repeatability of the innovation process. In recent times, Steve Jobs figured out how to innovate new products. He believed he could produce innovative products frequently and use his innovation process repeatedly.

Eventually, a repeatable innovation process had to be established, learned, and practiced routinely. Any process that becomes a routine leads to a new business function. About 20 percent of corporations have some type of innovation leader. This person may be called an innovation manager, director or chief innovation officer. We must learn and be on the edge of the curve in order to remain globally competitive. We must invest in educating our employees in innovation methods and practices. My research has shown that we also have to create incentives to produce a culture of learning employees. Reward success with an incentive for more learning.

We hear about market-driven innovation, open innovation, and research-and-development-driven (R&D) innovation. Every company must utilize all of these avenues. Research-and-development-driven innovation must be accelerated, market-driven innovation must be incorporated, and open innovation must be considered. The R&D-driven innovations give the perception of better control of intellectual property and take a longer time to implement. Market-driven innovations need to be developed quickly to take advantage of the shorter life opportunity. Open innovations cost money, like mergers and acquisitions, but they can be launched quickly. Thus, the innovation strategy for a corporation has to take into account all three drivers of innovation.

The Innovation Solution

Combining Eliyahu M Goldratt's theory of constraints and Six Sigma, I learned that in order for one to succeed, one must master the following four areas:

1. Time management

2. Process thinking

3. Statistical thinking

4. Innovative thinking

This finding established the need for people to learn to think innovatively. In an age of mass customization, we must be able to define the limits of the innovation process as innovation on demand and in real time—especially in service businesses. The question is: what should we be teaching? Further research showed that most of the innovation literature was about creativity, strategy, some singular aspect of innovation, corporate failures, or cases of corporate success.

The issue of achieving business growth through innovation was identified with the publication of the leading books on the topic—*The Innovator's Dilemma* and *The Innovator's Solution*. Since then, there has been significant dialogue about innovation. Many more books about innovation have been written; however, most literature still offers only past statistics about failures, strategies for success, and policies for innovation. These books do a great job of establishing a case for innovation, but offer limited innovation solutions.

While corporations such as Microsoft, Apple, Google, Proctor & Gamble, and IDEO keep the fire of innovation alive, many others continue to decline in the wake of competition from smaller, more innovative companies of the next generation. The generational gap between these new and old corporations is evident. New corporations are designed to innovate fast, while larger, older organizations need to build enough momentum to change before anything new can be accomplished.

The field of innovation science must answer questions about innovation, be easy to learn, and be empowering. The learning involved in innovation is not the accumulation of rote knowledge, nor is it totally prescriptive; rather, it must bring out the best in its users. Innovation cannot be taught using the conventional method of working with case studies alone. In order for people to act innovatively, they must be able to understand the science behind innovation, buy into it, practice it, and enjoy using it.

For executives to lead or require their staff to launch an innovation initiative effectively, they must first understand innovation science themselves so they can be actively and intellectually engaged anytime and enable the employees to innovate faster. Everyone has the capacity to be creative and innovative. The purpose of education in innovation, therefore, is to prepare and empower employees for more and faster innovation by applying creativity to deliver value to the customer. In order to make innovation meaningful, it must be significant enough to make a visible impact financially.

Thus to differentiate meaningful business innovations from less significant innovations, the framework for breakthrough innovation, Brinnovation, was created. The Brinnovation framework addresses the issues of how much innovation to have, what to innovate, how to create, and how to innovate. This framework requires the user to understand fully the difference between creativity and innovation.

My students at the Illinois Institute of Technology have helped me crystallize the difference between various key terms. *Creativity* is an idea; *invention* is about making it work once; and *innovation* is about reproducing the creative solution many times over for customers and getting paid for it. For example, iPod is considered a great innovation today. Now imagine if nobody bought an iPod. Would it still be called an innovation? In the absence of millions of customers, the iPod would more likely be called a creative product at best.

Let's look at the difference between an inventor and an innovator. Two distinct individuals or organizations play these roles in many cases. This arrangement takes away the first-mover advantage, because the innovator is often more informed about the pitfalls of the first innovation. For example, iPod is not the first MP3 player; the IBM computer is not the first desktop computer; Google is not the first search engine; and Microsoft is not the first operating system. Valuable lessons can be learned from initial mistakes, which are mostly seen by people other than the originator.

Given that innovation implies something very new, unique, or different, the Brinnovation framework provides a rule to quantify how much innovation is satisfactory. The *rule of two* states that breakthrough innovation means changing the effect or benefit of innovation by at least a factor of two. For example, no cell phone industry existed in the early eighties. No mobile phones were in use. The earliest mobile phone was as big as a backpack. The next version of a mobile phone was handheld (about the size of a brick). Soon, mobile phone models moved down in weight, size, and volume (about 15 percent a year). Then someone at Motorola suggested reducing the mobile phone by about 50 percent, thus surprising the competition. That decision led to the development of the famous "flip phone," and the cell phone industry was launched. The initial price for the phone was about three thousand dollars, and Motorola could not make enough of them.

For the next ten years or so, the average growth rate for the Motorola cell phone business was about 70 percent. Nokia, a new entrant into the cell phone market, later caught Motorola off guard. As the story goes, Motorola owned the market, so it did not care for the special and small order of digital phones (since it was minting money with analog phones). Nokia exploited the opportunity, launched digital phones, and captured market share. Motorola struggled and tried a variety of solutions. Then somebody internal suggested repeating what the company had done when it launched the flip phone.

At this time, Nokia phones were considered to be "candy bar" phones. Motorola decided to reduce the thickness of the phone by about 50 percent. This decision led to refining the design of the flip phone, and the new phone, called the Razr, priced at about five hundred dollars (while the benchmark phone was selling for thirty-nine dollars). Once again, Motorola could not make enough of their new phones. The challenge is always to sustain innovation rather than innovate only when you get in trouble.

Breakthrough innovation implies that if a solution is innovative, it better look innovative, feel innovative, work innovatively, and provide an enjoyable experience to the user. For example, the iPod replaced Sony's Discman. The iPod was smaller by more than 50 percent (divide by two when less is better), has more than twice the music capacity (multiply by two when more is better), and even reduces the price of your favorite song by more than 50 percent. After all, each CD probably has only one or two good songs on it, yet you pay for all eight or ten songs.

Similarly, the Brinnovation framework simplifies other innovation aspects, such as the types of innovations (i.e., fundamental, platform, derivative, and variation), and the way we think about innovations (i.e., good, crazy, stupid, and funny). Three steps to creativity, along with three steps to identify what to innovate, are presented in Brinnovation. There are four factors in the theory of innovation and five steps in the TEDOC (target, explore, develop, optimize, and commercialize) methodology for developing innovative solutions. Simply put, the Brinnovation framework brings all the various aspects of innovation together in a systematic manner thereby enabling executives to better realize and capitalize upon innovation's real and significant benefits in this age of knowledge.

What to Innovate?

For executives, the key question remains what to innovate. A company normally innovates in its own domain expertise, unless its innovators come into contact and collaborate with experts in other fields. The table below classifies a multitude of innovations in a set of categories. Most innovations will fall into the basic categories of human needs. The categories are safety, food, health, communication, productivity, entertainment and comfort as shown in figure 1.2.

One more category—the human desire to learn, discover, explore, and exploit—could be added to this list. For example, our missions to the moon and Mars, the development of particle physics, and sea explorations are examples of our human discoveries of natural treasures or phenomena for useful applications and innovations in the future.

Two Innovation Solutions

Microsoft's operating system and Office products, or Apple's iPods and other products have close to a billion customers. Microsoft products for personal productivity and iPods for personal entertainment are good examples of making creative solutions into great innovative products.

MICROSOFT SOFTWARE

Bill Gates and Paul Allen identified the two breakthrough technologies: ALTAIR, the hardware capable of supporting the programming language BASIC, and BASIC, the programming language capable of harnessing the limited computing power of ALTAIR. The merger of these breakthrough technologies laid the foundation that brought computing power from the confines of laboratories and research institutes into the home of the common person.

What makes Microsoft successful?

1. In the start-up phase, Microsoft was able to identify the commercial value of emerging technology and software.

2. Microsoft caused a paradigm shift in the operating system market when it introduced the GUI-based operating system Windows 95.

CATEGORY	PRODUCTS, SERVICES, OR SOLUTIONS
Safety	Photo chromatic glass, Electronic access card, Remotely operated bomb disposal unit, Metal detector, Airbags (Car)
Food	Microwave oven, Coffee maker, Tea bag, Frozen food, Zip lock bags, Jamba Juice, Organic food
Health	Safety razor, Electric toothbrush, Liquid bath soap, Blood sugar monitor, Heart rate monitor, Remote monitors
Communication	Webcam, Tube railway, Internet chat/video chatting application, Kneeling bus, Telephone, Wireless, iPhone, FedEx
Productivity	Photocopying machine, ATM, Vending machine, Drive-thru food joints, Coin operated shopping cart, Personal computer, Fax machine
Entertainment	Graphic user interface (GUI), Book reading software, Mouse, Streaming videos, iPod, iTouch, iPhone
Comfort	Body deodorant, Laptop, Revolving chair, Teflon, Microfiber towels, Wall projection clock, Car auto parking system

FIGURE 1.2 Categories of Innovation

3. Microsoft made heavy investments in research and development to create new technology breakthroughs.

4. Microsoft was able to identify the needs of enterprises and provide software that enabled a business entity to streamline its processes.

5. Microsoft has established platforms such as .NET on which independent software developers can develop customized applications.

APPLE IPOD

Tony Fadell, former employee of General Magic and Phillips, envisioned a small, hard-drive-based player linked with a content delivery system where users could legally obtain and download music. Fadell joined Apple in early 2001. He used PortalPlayer as the basis of the Apple player. The first iPods used five-gigabyte Toshiba hard drives that were the size of a quarter; ARM processors; an operating system from Pixo; a large, high-resolution display; a lithium polymer battery; and the most recognizable aesthetic feature of the device—the scroll wheel.

How did iPod become the popular product it is now?

The iPod was able to capture the digital music player market with its simple, easy-to-use interface and design. A new iPod model (called "generation" by Apple) is released every one and a half to two years and enjoys an already established customer base in the users of its earlier model. The iPod has graduated from a simple music player to a complete, handheld entertainment device capable of harnessing the Internet to deliver video game content. Apple has now introduced an iPod with a touch screen, giving the user an intuitive, natural way of interacting with the device like never before.

What made iPod successful?

1. Simplicity of design and functionality

2. High-quality end-user experience

3. Continued pursuit of innovation

4. Access to quality content to be used with the iPod

5. Reengineering of business processes in tune with the needs of the end users

6. Incremental innovation and further refinement of its current form

The Leadership for Innovation

Four of the most important leadership skills are honesty, knowledge, vision, and integrity. Leaders in their defined role must establish a vision of being a game changer, stretching oneself, and being futuristic. Having a good vision will require innovation. In financial terms, the vision must include achieving a certain level of profitable growth. This requires the use of innovation in everything. The vision begins with a personal commitment to be creative and recognize creativity in others. Creativity is the manifestation of the intellectual best of employees, and its absence demonstrates wasted intellectual resources. We must recognize that everyone is creative and can be innovative; therefore, going forward, we must provide structure, set expectations, and reward employees for applying creativity in their roles.

I have developed a three-step process to learn creativity. The steps are:

1. Make a commitment to be creative, always looking for a different way of doing things.

2. Start combining two or more items or ideas uniquely.

3. Make step 2 a subconscious habit, and learn to combine quickly.

At the leadership level, people who combine multiple approaches and ideas and implement new methods in organizational leadership toward the futuristic vision will energize employees. A growth-driven strategy creates fun at work; a cost-driven strategy causes stress. If employees are not having fun, they probably are not doing their best.

What can be innovated is within the domain of one's expertise, industry, and business focus. Ultimately, successful innovation must fulfill obvious or hidden human needs for safety, security, food, health, communication, productivity, socialization, or comfort. Typically, innovation opportunities show up as conflicts, inconveniences, stress, inconsistencies, challenges, or the waste of resources.

Following are three quick steps to determine what a person can innovate on the individual level. Deploying these steps as a group would speed up and maximize innovation.

1. Learn what you love to do (i.e., identify your innate skills). If they are buried too deep, you may have to think hard and reflect back into your childhood (all the way back to about the age of ten).

2. Continually look for opportunities for innovation.

3. Learn what the likely users of the innovation would love to experience. People love to pay more money for what they can enjoy (i.e., remember the iPod).

Chapter Two

A Strategy for Profitable Growth

In 1999, I was diversifying my business, and I jumped onto the dot-com bandwagon with the intent of experiencing it rather than just watching it go by. The knowledge I gained was tremendous. A lot of learning took place at a very steep price and in a very short time. It is difficult to judge whether it was the right or wrong decision, but in the end, I do not regret it. Here is the real story…

As I was building a dot-com business and raising money for the venture, everyone asked questions, such as: "How will you make money? What is the business model? Where is your business plan?" We hired an expert business plan writer based on a strong recommendation. He developed a great plan, but I could not understand it. Even though everyone knows that the business plan is just a plan, I was told, "Failure to plan is a plan to fail."

I had a business plan that I was trying to present to potential investors. I knew the follow-up question: "When will your business become profitable?" My dilemma on one hand was, if I showed the profit too soon, my need for money would be questioned, while, on the other hand, if I showed losses, then the business model would not seem like a good one. Given the success rate of about 10 - 20 percent for venture-capital-funded projects, I was not convinced that they knew any better.

I also noticed that profit and growth were considered to be mutually exclusive events. I did further research and found that when a company is focusing on growth, it usually sacrifices profit, and when a business is churning cash, it ignores investment in growth. Again, mergers and acquisitions are not considered successful business growth strategies, based on their poor success rate (about 17 percent, as stated in the last chapter).

The above experience led me to think, *why couldn't we pursue both profit and growth simultaneously?* I wondered about a corporation's fundamental strategy. Is it to make money? Making money was the strategy preached in the eighties and practiced religiously up until now by most corporations. At the same time, companies with records of long-term success, such as Proctor & Gamble, have been practicing a sound strategy for profit and growth. I concluded that the fundamental strategy for any business must be to *sustain profitable growth.* Committing to profitable growth instead of committing to either profit or growth leads to different approaches and tactics.

A strategy is a set of futuristic, sequential steps for achieving the desired performance targets utilizing given resources. Strategies must operate within the scope of the organization's vision. Tactics and procedures are used to implement the fundamental strategy. Organizations have multiple strategies in the areas of financing, marketing, operations, human resources, measurements, investments, improvement, and rewards, which positively affect quality, cost, productivity, and morale. All strategies must serve the strategy of achieving *sustained profitable growth (SPG).*

The Strategy for Execution (SFE) Map

A strategy for execution map (SFE) for a corporation begins with the fundamental strategy of sustained profitable growth. The strategy can be successfully executed and realize its full potential through four interrelated elements:

1. Measurements: Business scorecard

2. Profit improvement: Six Sigma / Lean methodologies

3. Business growth: Innovation

4. Sustenance: Process management

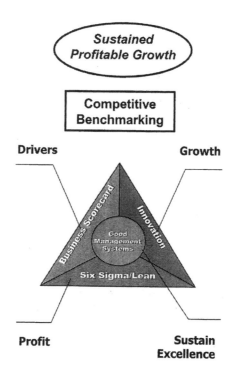

FIGURE 2.1 Strategy for Execution (SFE) Map

Without execution, a strategy is superfluous. It becomes nothing more than a fairy tale to be read. Merely developing a great strategy is like driving a car or flying a plane in your thoughts. You will keep going, but you will never get anywhere because there is no real movement. A disconnect between strategy and execution results in an uncoordinated effort. People within an organization with such a disconnect will run out of stamina, as the movement that they are making is for movement's sake only. Strategy is the guide, and execution is the engine. It is through the execution of a well-thought-out strategy that results are realized.

Continuing with the car analogy, if a company is running on all cylinders and has an interesting, compelling destination, the ability to execute is what will drive that company's success. Execution comes in the form of leadership, management, processes, understanding, measurement, and the desire to "roll up your sleeves" and get the "right" things done. Using corporate performance measurement tools, such as the Six Sigma Business Scorecard, movement toward the stated destination can be measured at any time.

Execution begins with a good set of measures, ensuring the realization of the fundamental strategy. The Six Sigma Business Scorecard measurements help achieve both profit and growth by identifying operational opportunities for improving profit, as well as pursuing innovation for achieving growth. Opportunities for profit improvement are addressed using tools like the Six Sigma and Lean principles. The increase in revenue growth is achieved through institutionalizing innovation principles. Innovation begins with an idea, and excellence in employee idea management will ensure the continual development of new products or services. The steps for executing a strategy to achieve sustained profitable growth are:

1. Commit to the fundamental strategy to achieve sustained profitable growth (SPG).

2. Utilize a strategy for execution map to accomplish SPG.

3. Perform a gap assessment using the Six Sigma Business Scorecard, and identify areas for improvement.

4. Establish the organization's vision, beliefs, goals, and initiatives (VBGI).

5. Construct a business processes flowchart, and identify critical processes and their measures of effectiveness. For example, in an engineering services business, proposal generation is a critical process, because the accuracy of estimates determines margins at the completion of the project.

6. Map the business scorecard elements to business processes.

7. Align the organization, establish responsibilities to accomplish the vision, and implement the Six Sigma Business Scorecard.

8. Measure and summarize data, display performance, and communicate expectations continually to all employees.

9. Identify elements of the business scorecard, as well as areas in the organization for actions necessary to impact profit and growth positively.

10. To improve profit, utilize tools like the Six Sigma DMAIC (define, measure, analyze, improve, and control) methodology or Lean principles.

11. To increase revenue growth, emphasize creativity and utilize the TEDOC (target, explore, develop, optimize, and commercialize) innovation methodology. A culture of innovation begins with excellence in idea management. Find ways to intellectually engage employees and encourage them to help develop new processes, products, or services.

12. Sustain improvement in business performance through the 4-P model of achieving process excellence (i.e., striving toward target performance at critical processes).

The SPG strategy serves the corporate purpose by matching business objectives with organization resources. The elements of this strategy have uncertainties associated with them. For example, predicting how people will end up performing a certain task and determining the customers' response to a certain product or service are difficult. Even more difficult is predicting market acceptance of a certain product or service offered by a company. This difficulty, however, can be minimized by pursuing business innovation correctly. Thus, a good strategy must take into account the available resources and drive corporate performance in a predicted direction in spite of given uncertainties. If not taken into consideration, these uncertainties can cause strategies to fail, as they are not often anticipated in formulating scenarios.

We have all experienced (some more than others) the impact of the senior executive strategy meetings, where executives venture out to shape the future of their enterprises and return with a high-level plan for the future. However, the real work begins with the integration of this newly established plan into the rest of the organization.

Much like the old conundrum, "Which came first: the chicken or the egg?" a similar situation arises here, "Which comes first: strategy or execution?" While strategy clearly has to drive execution, many feel that results in the field do not support this viewpoint. Academia, authors, and corporate leaders alike recognize that organizations can have excellent strategic plans, but they are rarely executed successfully.

Organizational Alignment

An individual's ability to execute is finite, while a team's ability to do so is greatly multiplied. A team gets things done far more effectively than an individual. Simply put, when properly coordinated, a team brings different points of view, skill sets, and unlimited energy to achieve any specific goal.

The challenge with the team (and this can be extrapolated to an entire organization), however, is that unless its members are in alignment, their ability to achieve the goal is at risk. Consider the following transportation example. A ten-member team must navigate from Boston, Massachusetts, USA, to Sydney, Australia. How will team members execute this task? What obstacles are in their way? What resources do they have available to them? Different people on the team will have different ideas of how to get the job done.

If the team cannot realize "true" alignment on how to get there, members will end up taking different forms of transportation. Members may even go in totally different directions to get to Sydney (i.e., some will go west while others will go east). Without any measures (e.g., how long it should take) to guide them, the team may not fulfill its charter in an effective manner. Therefore, the team members need to get themselves aligned on the best way to achieve the goal.

"True" alignment is important, because what some team members agree to during planning is not always the way they execute the plan. Cultural differences and discrepancies in understanding can cause this mismatch, but it is more about people saying one thing and doing something else based primarily on their own personal self-interest. At the end of the day, if the team is not aligned on what to do and how to get it done, then the effort it takes to get the job done (if it gets done at all) will be much greater than with "true" alignment. One can envision nine members of a ten-person team waiting in Sydney for the last team member to show up;

they have no idea where this person is or how this person might be arriving. The reality is that until the last member of the team shows up, the job is not complete!

A Roadmap to Profitable Growth

In 2001, Robert Kaplan and David Norton introduced strategy maps to establish the cause-and-effect logic connecting strategic outcomes with the drivers. In their book *The Strategy-Focused Organization*, the authors state, "A Balanced Scorecard Strategy Map is a generic architecture for describing a strategy." The fundamental objective of designing various strategies is to increase shareholder value. Therefore, a roadmap to execute a strategy must lead to realizing the intended objective of profitable growth, which results in higher shareholder value.

The roadmap to profitable growth begins with a performance assessment followed by the clearly established corporate vision, beliefs, goals, and initiatives aligned with the fundamental strategy. Six Sigma and Lean-type tools can be used aggressively to achieve excellence in operations and improve profit. Breakthrough innovation tools can be used to achieve revenue growth.

In the case of Six Sigma, the focus must be on its intent, which is to accelerate improvement. The statistical thinking is more important than using the advanced statistical tools. Brinnovation highlights the need to understand innovation before starting to measure it. The basic building block of innovation is a "networked individual" with unlimited potential for innovation. The Brinnovation methodology must ensure all five phases of TEDOC (target, explore, develop, optimize, and commercialize) are deployed for accelerating and maximizing innovation.

The discussion on strategy for profitable growth highlights the need to deploy the fundamental strategy (SPG) and execute it effectively. These goals are accomplished by focusing on value-added business processes and assigning clear responsibilities. The objective is to make strategy much more successful than the 10 percent generally reported.

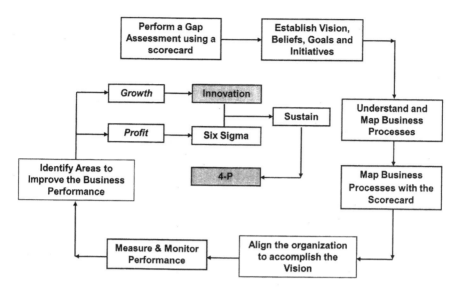

FIGURE 2.2 A Roadmap to Profitable Growth

Chapter Three

Breakthrough Innovation Framework

Striving for immortality or comfortable circumstances drives the human mind to innovate better ways to live. The innovation can be in the areas of drugs, foods, tools, communication, or even astronomy. At the extreme, the drive to innovate originates from a fear of extinction, while on a more prosaic level, it arises out of the desire to make life more comfortable or free from suffering. The focus of successful innovation is to fulfill human needs, which include health, food, work, communication, security, and knowledge. Any drug for longevity, delicious food for better health, instrument for earning a salary, device to communicate faster, weapon to protect, or method of knowledge acquisition to perpetuate an appetite for more will lead to commercially successful innovations, if they are affordable.

Peter Drucker[1] observed that the innovation must be purposeful and begin with an analysis of the opportunities. Accordingly, the innovation must also be simple and capable of performing at least one specific task. He

---

1   Drucker, 2002.

further identifies seven sources of innovation that include a flash of genius, exploiting incongruity or contradiction, growth in demand, changes in demographics or perceptions, and creating new knowledge. Recent knowledge innovations include history-makers, such as the personal computer, cellular phone, iPod, hybrid, and the Internet; earlier such innovations include the airplane, wireless technology, electricity, cement, penicillin, and so on. Finally, innovation encompasses the discoveries in space, like new planets, and development of new materials, such as previously unknown elements like Uranium. These innovations universally required commitment, hard work, and perseverance.

In the early stages of the use of electricity, corporations used to have chief electricity officers; in the information age, businesses appointed chief information officers; now, in the knowledge age, businesses are frequently appointing innovation officers. Innovation is moving toward becoming a standard process similar to other functions in business, such as purchasing, sales, or quality control. Becoming a standard process implies a standard task must be performed; the outcome is predictable to some extent; personnel are designated for the process; a box exists for it on the organization chart; and a room in the facility is set aside and labeled for it.

Similarly, as the innovation process moves toward becoming a standard process, people must designate a particular space for innovation; personnel must be assigned to innovation; an innovation box must exist on the organization chart; and someone must assume the role of chief innovation officer. Some companies have already appointed innovation chiefs, including Coca-Cola of the United States, DSM of the Netherlands, the Health Science Centre in Canada, Publicis Groupe Media of France, and Mitsubishi and Hitachi of Japan, implying their focus and resource commitment to innovation in sustaining profitable growth.

Companies like 3M, Proctor & Gamble, AT&T, IBM, Siemens, Sony, Toshiba, Airbus, Unilever, Ford, GM, Tata, and Birla have been innovating for many years. Even large corporations, however, are realizing that the innovation process utilized thus far may not be as effective or competitive as it was in the past. IBM offers innovation-on-demand consulting services to other businesses, yet even experts at IBM are realizing that their current understanding of innovation needs improvement.

In 2004, IBM organized the Global Innovation Outlook (GIO), which initiated a global dialogue on learning and the changing nature of innovation. Participants included representatives of academia, the government, non-government organizations, corporations, venture-capital firms, think tanks and various experts. The GIO reports that up until this point, business must have mistaken invention for innovation. One of the more obvious recent changes is that innovation is occurring much faster.

Participants of the GIO consequently recognized the need to redefine innovation. Accordingly, the consensus opinion was that "We must define twenty-first century innovation as beginning at the intersection of invention and insight: We innovate when a new thought, business model, or service actually changes society." This redefinition of innovation demonstrates that businesses must adjust their understanding of innovation in the knowledge age.

When comparing innovation in the twentieth century with innovation in the twenty-first century, we see that in the twentieth century, innovation was a forte of large corporations with tremendous resources for research and development. The smaller corporations followed their lead by developing derivative products. New knowledge had protection from reuse without compensation. Large corporations grew and employed thousands of people. The standard of living improved, and families saved money. At some point, when risk was manageable, entrepreneurs tried something new related to their work at larger corporations, and the idea spun off. New companies formed and grew to become larger corporations. However, the new large corporations did not fund the basic research and development like their predecessors did as they could not afford to continue such practices.

In the twenty-first century, however, knowledge acquisition has been decentralized through the invention of the Internet. People have access to knowledge anywhere there is access to the Internet. With the Internet, the formerly concentrated control of knowledge has fragmented all the way down to individuals. As a result, the rate of innovation is changing, and large corporations cannot keep up with it. Many new companies start up with fresh ideas funded by the resources of venture-capital firms. Therefore, larger corporations must recognize this new model of innovation. Some large firms, like Proctor & Gamble, have set goals to seek a certain percentage of innovation from outside the corporation's boundaries. Such outsourcing of innovation is called "open innovation."

An examination of the innovations of the last century highlights the amazing degree of change that has occurred—from horse cart to space shuttle, labor to automation, material flow to information flow, and physical resources to intellectual resources. Physical resources include time and material, while intellectual resources imply knowledge. Figure 3.1 shows a comparison of innovation in the age of time and material with that of the knowledge age in terms of material, machines, methods, people, skills, testing instruments, and the environment.

KEY RESOURCES	TIME AND MATERIAL/ PHYSICAL AGE	INFORMATION/ KNOWLEDGE AGE
Material	Raw material	Information
Tools	Machines and tools	*Brain (to be understood)*
Methods	Repeatable Processes for well understood machines	*Repeatable process to be developed*
People	Workers for physical effort	Workers with thinking effort
Environment	Comfortable for producing goods	Learning and creative
Expectation	High volume reproducible products	High volume customized solutions
Measurements	Productivity and Performance	Performance and productivity

FIGURE 3.1 Ages of Innovation

For the innovation process to be repeatable and available for any innovator, from the individual to larger corporations, some standard process must be established. In order for the innovation process to become repeatable, it must first be understood. To understand the innovation process, a basic framework must be uncovered, which can then be used to fill in the blanks for producing a repeatable innovation process. The process must work with any brain, be easy to understand, and be logical enough for many people to use it repeatedly.

In the knowledge age, with access to the Internet, a networked individual is the building block of innovation. As shown in Figure 3.2, now the individual has access way beyond the network of a few individuals; instead, practically the whole world is the network. Once the network really becomes ubiquitous, the individual has access to laboratories, universities, experts, corporations, and trademark and patent offices. This phenomenon has already begun; however, its full impact is yet to be realized.

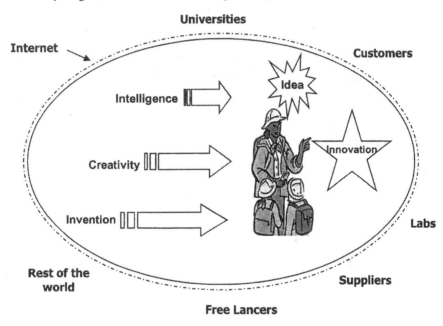

FIGURE 3.2 Building Block of Innovation

Once the building block of innovation is established, defining the concept of innovation becomes equally important. Creativity and innovation are often used interchangeably; however, experts define innovation as the process by which a creative idea is applied to produce value to society. The current process of innovation goes from idea to commercialization. Until the idea becomes a financial success, it remains just a creative idea. Once the creative idea becomes successful, however, it becomes a major breakthrough—an innovation.

In the knowledge age, we need to utilize the processes of both Einstein and Edison to produce knowledge solutions. Einstein helped us learn about the theory of innovation, and Edison helped us understand the methodology of solution development. Interestingly, Einstein did no physical experiments, while Edison had laboratories and the innovation room for developmental experiments. Einstein believed that every innovation is discovered, and Edison believed innovation could be produced on demand. Innovation thus becomes the discovery of an innovative solution on demand. With this understanding, we can develop a framework and establish a methodology.

Innovative Thinking

The Einstein exhibits in the Boston Museum of Science show that most of his innovative work was published in four papers in 1905. Einstein tried to put the puzzle together with various pieces of nature, which he then tried to include in his unsuccessful effort to develop a unifying theory. Even with the availability of various innovation methodologies, tools, and practices, a framework for innovative thinking was yet to be developed. Without such a framework, the predictability of methodologies and the repeatability of the innovation process could not be established with confidence. I have developed a model called Gupta's Einsteinian theory of innovation (GETI) to provide this needed framework for innovation.

GETI is based on Einstein's famous equation $E = mc^2$, where the "E" represents energy, the "m" represents mass, and the "c" represents the speed of light. Einstein's equation delineates the relationship inherent in the conversion between mass and energy. Every activity in nature is a conversion process.

Human beings are also energy converters. People consume resources and convert energy. Energy conversion can be physical or intellectual. The intellectual burning of energy occurs through thinking. When a person is thinking, his or her ability to focus or channel energy in a direction, start associating various experiences with one another, and generate thoughts based upon those associations is critical. Thinking is continual; it is purposeful or inadvertent. When people think inadvertently, their thoughts float through randomly; when purposefully thinking, people channel their thinking in some direction to get an answer.

Thus, innovation begins with an idea, which is an outcome of the thinking process; it must have some energy associated with it. Sometimes, a lot of energy is required to think of an idea for a particular purpose. People even literally scratch their heads to stir up and stimulate thinking. Thus, every idea must have some energy associated with it that is an outcome of effort and the speed of the thought.

All discoveries occur in the human brain. Certain parts of the brain contribute to the innovation process. The brain has a cortex that consists of billions of neurons (cells) and trillions of axons (connectors). Neurons and axons form connections called synapses. With billions of neurons and trillions of axons, the number of possible synapses is practically infinite. The way the brain continually processes information is by comparing stored and received information. The speed of thought refers to how fast the brain can process the information stored and received, thus generating an idea.

Imagine a patch of cortex consisting of 75 x 30 neurons as shown in figure 3.3. In order to match object A with an object A', the brain could compare one cell at a time to see if the objects match. Such a process may take thousands of comparisons. However, an experienced mind that has built anchors can quickly hop from object A to object A' and make the match. Such a comparison can take about five milliseconds. Stated another way, if the brain has to make thousands of comparisons, it can take hours, but if the brain can hop through the anchors, it can make comparisons quickly.

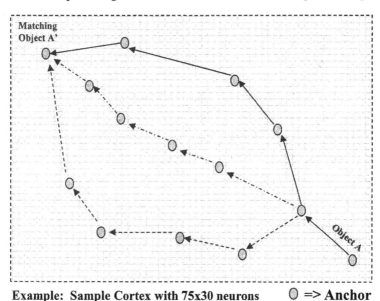

Example: Sample Cortex with 75x30 neurons   ◎ => **Anchor**

FIGURE 3.3 Speed of Thinking

The numbers or matching time could be astronomical—practically forever—if the person makes comparisons one cell at a time. The speed of thought, however, can be accelerated by installing anchors based on multidisciplinary experiences. The actual brain speed can be one synapse per five milliseconds. However, since the brain has billions of neurons and trillions of axons, billions or trillions of synapses can form in parallel within five milliseconds. Moreover, if the anchors already exist, the speed can increase.

As to the comparison with the speed of light, the speed of thought can be much faster if the anchor is already established in the brain for two points, irrespective of their distance. If a person has been on the moon or somewhere light years away, the brain can hop to that location right away in the mind on demand. Interestingly, the capacity of the brain is practically infinite with respect to visualizing the universe. Richard Restak, MD, in his book *Brainscapes*, mentioned that the number of synapses is about 10^{80} and that number is considered to be the same as the number of atoms in the universe. The brain can handle many objects, perform associations, discover new things, and innovate.

Thus, an innovation is a transformation of one set of ideas into another set of more productive ideas. The speed at which a person can process these thoughts becomes an important factor in accelerating or creating innovation on demand. Applying Einstein's equation to the process of innovation, one can equate "E" to the energy (value) associated with innovation, "m" to the physical effort or resources allocated to innovation, and "c" to the speed of thought, which can be faster than the speed of light. Restating Einstein's equation with proper substitutions, GETI delineates the following relationship:

Innovation Value = Resources x (Speed of Thought)^2

Where, the speed of thought can be described by the following relationship:

Speed of Thought $\equiv$ Function (Knowledge, Play, Imagination)

The units of the innovation value can be represented in terms of resources and ideas over the unit of time, which can be equated to a new unit, Einstein (E), with the maximum value of "1." Thus, the innovation value can be increased with more resources or faster generation and processing of ideas. The innovation value accelerates with better utilization of intellectual resources rather than the mere allocation more physical resources.

RESOURCES (R)	KNOWLEDGE (K)	PLAY (P)	IMAGINATION (I)	INNOVATION VALUE (IV)	COMMENT
Degree of resources or time committed	Extent of knowledge based on research and experience	Percentage (%) of possible combinations of various variables explored	Dimension extrapolated as a percentage of ideal solution for breakthrough improvement	Estimated Innovation Level	This is an initial estimation of the proposed model. Further work is required.
50% (Limited time and insufficient resources)	75% (Significant knowledge and experience gained, some latest work is to be explored)	40% (Percentage of combination of variables explored mentally, experimentally or through simulation. Work is in progress)	66% (Selected dimension is extrapolated such that improvement is expected to be about 30%, which is about 66% of the breakthrough improvement)	0.182 (Long way to find an innovative solution due to lack of effort and play. To accelerate, one needs to improve all elements of innovation.)	Innovation Value = 0.5x((0.75+0.4+ 0.66)/3)² =0.182 Einstein

FIGURE 3.4 Using GETI for Assessing Personal Innovation

Figure 3.4 defines various terms and gives an example of the quantification of personal innovation.

In other words, the innovation value is equal to the resources (commitment) times a function of knowledge, play, and imagination (KPI) squared. More than its numerical value, the equation identifies elements of innovation in order to maximize the innovation value. Most innovations are based on research, current experiments, and innovative thinking. Measuring knowledge and quantifying combinatorial play are possible, but measuring imagination is difficult because of the complexity of mental processes. Therefore, imagination is transformed in quantifiable terms by understanding that *pure imagination is a random extrapolation*. Thus, imagination becomes a measurable component by the nature of extrapolation.

Innovation Categories

After reviewing contributions of several great innovators, specifically Einstein, Galileo, and Edison, we can see that Einstein engaged in mostly theoretical innovations, Edison innovated practical or business solutions, and Galileo did a combination of both. Einstein's work was fundamental in nature, while Edison's work was more tangible. Einstein conducted mostly thought experiments, e.g. riding the light wave, while Edison conducted hands-on experiments in his laboratory. Understanding types of innovations and their relevance to a business helps in establishing appropriate goals for innovations and devising correct measures of innovation. Innovation on demand can mean different things to different levels of innovation. Looking at various innovations, we can classify them into four categories based on the amount of effort and the speed-of-thought component. The four categories of innovations are the following:

1. Fundamental
2. Platform
3. Derivative
4. Variation

The *fundamental* innovation is a creative idea that leads to a revolution in ways of thinking. Such innovations are based on extensive research; they are extremely knowledge driven and theoretically proven and lead to follow-up research and development. Such innovations occur with the collaborations of academia, commercial laboratories, and even corporations. The fundamental innovations may lead to changes in the way we think about some aspect of human existence, extend an existing theory, or be breakthrough concepts with enormous impact, perhaps leading to the evolution of a new industry.

In fact, such innovations contribute to human evolution. Examples include Einstein's theory of relativity, light quanta or photons, electricity, penicillin, the telephone, Xerox, wireless communication, the transistor, computer software, UNIX, the Internet, the fractal, the Edison effect, and planes. Science, usually from the academic arena, is a significant component of the fundamental innovation, which makes it available for the common good and thus less commercially protected.

The *platform* innovation is defined as one that leads to the practical application of fundamental innovations. Such innovations normally are launching pads for a new industry. Examples of platform innovations include personal computers, silicon chips, cell phones, digital printers, Web technology, Microsoft Windows, databases, CDMA, Linux, drug-delivery devices, satellites, and the space shuttles. The platform component increases the portion of the laboratory or development component compared to the fundamental innovations. Platform innovations launch industries, change people's way of living, and fulfill the basic purpose of innovation, which is to help people live longer and more comfortably.

The *derivative* innovation is a secondary product or service derived from a platform innovation. Derivative innovations include new server-client configurations based on the new network architecture or operating system for a cell phone, for example. Derivative innovations are slight modifications of the main product. In the case of Microsoft-like software, the platform is Windows, and derivatives are a new office suite; for CDMA-like platforms, derivative innovations are various features available to service providers; and for a major satellite system, the derivative innovations are various launching options or capabilities offered to users.

The *variation* innovation is the tertiary level of innovation, which requires much less time and is a slight variation of the next-level products or services based on the derivative innovations. For example, variation innovations in cell phones are various color covers, ringtones, camera features, and more software-based optional features. In the case of Microsoft software, variation innovations are various applications developed and based on the Microsoft platform and derivative innovations. Typically, the variation innovation occurs close to the customer. It may be the best candidate for reaching the ultimate in speed of innovation or innovation on demand in real time.

Understanding types of innovations and their relevance to a business helps in establishing appropriate goals for innovation and devising correct measures of innovation. Figure 3.5, "Attributes of Innovation," lists various aspects of innovation. Innovation on demand can mean different things to different levels of innovation.

Over time, responsibilities with regard to where to allocate resources and who can reposition such resources must be made clear. For example, switching systems, chip-manufacturing facilities, and basic material or technology research have gone beyond the affordability of businesses; their collaboration with one another, or the government's support, has to come into the picture to further the fundamental or platform innovation. Based on the commercial success of an innovation, the innovation can move to the next level up or higher. For example, a cell phone like the Razor (Motorola), which becomes very successful, can become a platform in itself (rather than a derivative innovation of a larger strategy). Microsoft Office is a platform innovation based on its success.

TYPES OF INNOVATION	PRIMARY DRIVERS	KEY ASPECTS	DELIVERABLES	FREQUENCY	TIME TO INNOVATE	OWNERSHIP
Fundamental	University/ Laboratories	Science/ Knowledge	Concepts/ Revelations	Rare	Years – Months	Govt. (s)
Platform	Corporate R&D	Technology/ Large Sys.	Equipment/ Capability	Sporadic	Months – Weeks	Govt./ Business
Derivatives	In-house/ Outsourced	Application/ Small Sys.	Product/ Service	Regular	Weeks – Days	Business/ Individuals
Variations	Networks/ Individuals	Disposables/ Ideas	Packaging/ Integration	Continuous	Days – On-demand	Individuals

FIGURE 3.5 Attributes of Innovation

Many additional, diverse, next-tier products or applications can be developed from this platform.

Various types of innovations are achieved with differing degrees of the speed of thought. For example, a fundamental innovation may require a more meditative process to come up with the theories, concepts, or solutions without major experimentation. In fundamental innovation, knowledge and imagination are the key components. As mentioned earlier, most of Einstein's work was completed in his mind rather than in a laboratory. He typically conducted "thought experiments."

The platform innovation involves relatively less knowledge and imagination and more play or experimentation. Figure 3.6, "The Speed of Thought versus Type of Innovation," shows that variation innovation requires more play or more development effort than research and reflection. The chart helps in understanding how various innovators focus on a particular area for their work and various innovations are achievable by focusing on the right component of the speed of thought. In reality, the speed of thought becomes the manifestation of the speed (or rate) of innovation.

Figure 3.7, "The Extent of Innovation," shows that fundamental innovations can take a much longer time than variation innovations. As a result, more variation innovations will be produced than fundamental innovations. A fundamental innovation is a rarity, while variation innovations are continuously occurring.

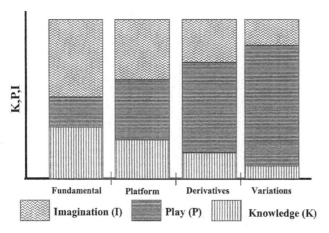

FIGURE 3.6 Speed of Thought Elements vs. Type of Innovation

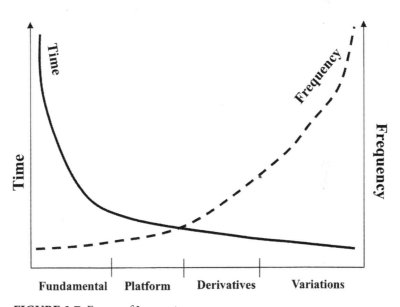

FIGURE 3.7 Extent of Innovation

The Breakthrough Innovation Process

Figure 3.8 graphically depicts the innovation process, which, at first glance, appears to be linear. However, any step within the linear process has nested loops or divergences. As an overall process, the innovation process must be streamlined and appear linear in order to show progress. This process is based upon the Brinnovation framework and is designed to produce innovation on demand. In other words, innovation begins with a demand, and it must be purposeful.

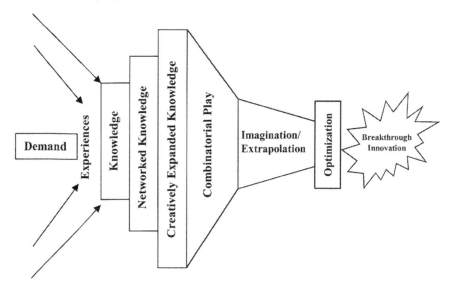

FIGURE 3.8 Brinnovation™ Methodology

The first step of the innovation process is to listen to the requirements for innovation and then gather knowledge about the topic in order to identify the necessary inputs to the innovation. The networked individual, or the innovator, gathers more knowledge to achieve a certain level of competency in the field quickly. At this stage, process thinking helps to identify appropriate input for the intended innovative solution. This step is a critical one and is missing from the current methods of innovation, where an innovator searches for a solution or the outcome.

The following steps summarize the basic innovation process, which can be used to realize breakthrough solutions through innovative thinking:

1. Understand the need for innovation and its purpose. Research a topic individually, collectively, and through the networked resources, to gain a deeper understanding of the subject. Do not immediately solve the problem without proper research and knowledge.

2. Identify the potential variables affecting the problem. Make the list as long as possible and expand it using creativity tools, such as benchmarking, brainstorming, mind mapping and TRIZ, a Russian acronym for Theory of Inventive Problem Solving.

3. Test "what if" scenarios to isolate unlikely combinations of variables and identify likely combinations of variables. The objective is to remove obviously unrelated variables and retain related innovative solutions.

4. Establish the dimension of improvement or the performance characteristic(s).

5. Investigate likely combinations that could improve the performance characteristic(s).

6. Extrapolate the dimensions of interest and validate potential outcomes.

7. Expand your thinking by applying appropriate TRIZ-like principles to help you explore potential innovative solutions for generating significant change, thus making innovation obvious or disruptive.

8. Continue to explore and formulate alternative solutions. Select a solution that produces expected breakthrough improvement for further validation, optimization, and implementation.

The Brinnovation approach to developing an innovative solution is more systematic and much faster than searching for a solution among millions of possibilities. The current process of innovation appears to be an art, a random occurrence, or a flash of genius because of the frequency of its occurrence and the unpredictability associated with the search pattern. Some people, who have mastered the innovation process, become serial innovators, while those people who do not understand the process they rarely conceive innovative ideas.

The idea generation process in the current environment focuses on ideas on the potential solutions and then picks the one that justifies the use of resources for a tryout or its novelty. The Brinnovation process of innovation, however, incorporates a system for creativity or divergence and innovative convergence. The planned convergence process, or an algorithm associated with it, can speed up the innovation process, so you are able to identify causative sources of innovation. Once the purpose and causes of innovation are identified, then the extrapolation is utilized to achieve the desired extent of innovation.

The current process of imagination focuses more on subtle aspects, such as visualization, dreaming, or using the subconscious mind. If a person is introspective, the current process of imagination can be described as the ability to imagine various possibilities. In order to understand the imagination process better, it is necessary to look at its boundary condition, which is pure imagination.

Pure imagination appears to be conceiving very random thoughts or possible solutions and then playing with them in the mind by stretching them to their limits. Typically, when people imagine and stretch, they tend to go to the ultimate limits, which are beyond business needs. People imagining to that extreme often get lost and forget the purpose of innovation as well as lose their train of thought. Thus, innovation on demand requires purposeful imagination. Purposeful imagination is the identification of practical solutions and the extrapolation of the best solution in the direction of innovation.

Innovative Idea Generation

One of the challenges in developing innovative solutions is mastering the practice of innovative thinking. In many brainstorming sessions, most of the ideas appear to be in the line of "been there, done that," nothing new, or "same old, same old." Many ideas or suggestion programs fail because of the triviality or the purposelessness of the ideas. Most people do not even consider themselves innovative individuals. Even the perceived "dumbest" mind has enough neurons and axons for truly innovative thought. In order to stimulate the thinking of the average human, I have developed a process, which because of its simplicity, at first glance, may be perceived as trivial but is actually quite powerful. In the many sessions I have conducted, I have demonstrated that this simple process works.

The first step is to clear the mind. Asking people to write down good ideas about a topic without talking to other people is an important part of achieving this state. People love this step; they already have so many good ideas clogging their minds. Once these ideas are written down, the mind is open, biases are out, and resistance is down. Upon review, you will find that most of these ideas are of the "same old" variety; they are ideas people have already thought of and found to be useless.

Having cleared the mind of these ideas, people can be asked to write crazy ideas about the same topic. "Crazy" here is defined as stretching the mind logically by thinking about what can be done to the subject of innovation at its extremes. The left hemisphere of the brain usually drives the crazy thinking. These ideas stretch current performance levels. People will often continue with the "good idea" process; thus, many of their "crazy" ideas still look like "good" old ideas. Many people really struggle to conceive crazy ideas.

The next step is to involve the right hemisphere of the brain by asking participants to write down stupid ideas. "Stupid" ideas here represent what many would consider unintelligent ideas, which really are unrelated to the subject. Participants see the difficulty in conceiving stupid ideas, and they learn to appreciate them (as they really are well-thought-out, innovative ideas).

The right hemisphere of the brain usually drives spatial thinking, which broadens the scope of innovation. This thinking represents the creative aspects of innovation. People are afraid of thinking this way for fear of being called "stupid" themselves. They must recognize that stupid ideas can be innovative ideas, as can some of the unlikeliest possible combinations of variables. At this stage, practically everyone tries to avoid looking "stupid"; however, with enough prodding, participants can be coaxed to generate a few such ideas. The objective here is to learn to think innovatively by utilizing all available mental resources and gaining speed of thought through the practice of thinking. Some people are good at thinking of stupid ideas. Such individuals have a sense of uniqueness and differentiation.

At this point, people have learned to apply thinking on demand (i.e., they have developed flexibility of thinking). Mental agility is fundamental to developing the ability to think of innovative ideas quickly. The final step in this process is to write down funny ideas about the subject of interest for innovation. Here, practically everyone stumbles, with only a few exceptions. People have to think hard to come up with funny ideas. The innovation process looks like improvisation. At this stage, people are practicing combinatorial play, or freely trying to associate various things they know about the subject of innovation.

After reviewing several sessions in which participants applied the above process, I discovered that idea generation does take time. Generating innovative ideas takes even more time than generating good ideas. As figure 3.9, "Innovative Thinking" shows, the funny ideas take the most time of all but are also more innovative than good ideas.

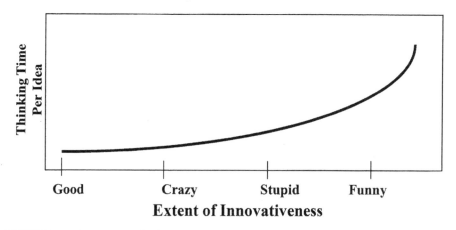

FIGURE 3.9 Innovative Thinking

Many leaders want their employees to have fun at work and try to communicate this to them. However, measuring whether employees have fun at work is difficult. The objective is not just to have fun, but to have fun productively. Learning to come up with funny ideas demonstrates what can become a measure of having fun at work. Having fun means employees feel free to give such ideas without any fear of ridicule or retribution. The quantity of purposeful, funny ideas is a great measure of the innovative thinking of an organization's human capital.

Henry Chesbrough, in his book *Open Innovation*, talks about the shift in the paradigm of innovation from R&D-driven, closed innovation to open innovation. Accordingly, open innovation recognizes the value created by innovation outside the boundaries of an organization. The closed innovation model focuses mainly on internal sources for innovation, while the open innovation model utilizes the best resources available regardless of where they originate. In today's economy, businesses should deploy both internal and external resources to speed up innovation. Open innovation incorporates external ideas and internal resources to create value.

Brinnovation utilizes open innovation and external sources to gain knowledge and ideas, and internal competencies to create value from the ideas. External resources enhance the creative component through networked research and benchmarking, and internal resources develop an innovative solution from the resulting input. The purpose of Brinnovation is to accelerate the frequency of breakthrough solutions in an open innovation environment, while still maximizing the use of the available intellectual resources of the human capital.

The Brinnovation framework is based on the experiences of the best innovators, including Einstein, Edison, Galileo, Newton, and Ford. The process is less dependent on an individual flash of genius and more dependent on access to the available knowledge at work. As a result, any individual can become innovative if he or she practices the process of innovation. The framework of innovation identifies the components of innovation and enhances the person's understanding of the innovation process, which eventually will lead to a more robust process. The challenge is in accepting that everyone can be innovative and produce innovative solutions on demand.

Chapter Four

The TEDOC Methodology

The topic of innovation is a frequently discussed one. It is on almost every CEO's agenda. The definition of innovation, how it differs from creativity, innovation methodologies, measures of innovation, innovation strategies, and, of course, the types of innovation are all subjects of ongoing debates. The first step in pursuing innovation is to understand what type of innovation a company needs and how much resources a company should commit to developing a systematic innovation practice.

Types of Innovation

OUTCOME-BASED INNOVATIONS

One common category of innovation is outcome-based innovation, which is comprised of the incremental, radical, and general-purpose types of innovation. Incremental innovation indicates a continual improvement of an existing product, process, service, or solution. Radical innovation represents the replacement of an existing solution with a significantly different approach (e.g., a transistor replacing vacuum tubes in electronics or e-mail replacing conventional mail). A radical innovation causes a disruption in the current way of doing things. General-purpose innovation describes significant innovations that fundamentally change ways of thinking and doing. Such innovations have a wide impact, a big scope of improvement, and a broader range of uses (e.g., the discovery of electricity or Einstein's theory of relativity).

PROCESS-BASED INNOVATIONS

Four categories of innovation are defined by their process—continuous process improvement, process revolutions, product or service innovations, and strategic innovations. Continuous process improvement innovations include methodologies such as Lean. The focus is on incremental innovations. Process revolutions relates to the implementation of new technology, such as RFID, for improving supply-chain management productivity. Product or service innovations represent new products or services, such as the iPhone, without changing business models. Strategic innovations include new products or services, but with new business models such as Segway rentals or Web-based applications.

OPERATIONS-BASED INNOVATIONS

Some organizations differentiate between types of innovation based on the subject area. According to the Doblin Group, there are four categories of innovations including finance, process, offerings, and delivery. Finance innovation relates to business models, networks, and alliances for innovations such as Dell's personal computer business and supply-chain management. Process innovation relates to enabling processes for innovations, such as the compensation and benefits packages at Starbucks and real-time inventory management at Wal-Mart. Offerings innovations include product performance enhancements through unique features, such as in an automobile or Microsoft Office, and service extras as seen in Singapore Airlines flights. Delivery innovations include improvements in channel (e.g., Martha Stewart products), brands (e.g., the iPod), and customer experience (e.g., Harley Davidson).

PATHWAY-BASED INNOVATIONS

The four types of pathway-based innovations are product, process, positioning, and paradigm. Product innovations are most apparent in the mobile phone market, with new phones arriving frequently. Process innovations include new methodologies, such as Six Sigma, Lean, and TRIZ. Positioning innovation implies repackaging an existing product or service and branding it innovatively (e.g., the increasing camera capabilities of cell phones could lead to them being branded as cameras). Paradigm innovation represents a shift in thinking and doing. For example, mainframe computers in the late 1970s led to the personal computer, a new paradigm of computing. Today, mobile phones are making conventional landline phones obsolete, and Internet phones are in some cases replacing mobile phones.

HIERARCHY-BASED INNOVATIONS

In order to build a portfolio of innovations—and have a strong causative relationship between innovation and allocated resources—a variety of innovations can be classified in a hierarchical manner. Depending upon the primary responsibility for managing innovation and key steps in the innovation process, the following innovation types are possible: business model, managerial, process, service, and product. Of these types of innovation, the business model is the most critical, as it sets the direction and the approach of a corporation. Managerial innovation relates to innovative approaches to managing people, technology, and resources. Process innovation implies a revolutionary improvement to, or reengineering of, an existing activity. Service innovation means developing new ways to deliver services or creating altogether new services. Product innovation involves creating products that offer new capabilities for significant economic payoff.

ACTIVITY-BASED INNOVATIONS

While all of the previously defined classifications have their merits, fundamentally speaking, innovation is an intellectual activity. Creativity is a unique combination of two events or ideas—the ability to discover the unique combination is critical. Applied creativity is innovation. The breadth of an organization's creativity is controlled by people, influenced both by the environment and opportunities provided by a company's leadership.

Upon reviewing the contributions of the great innovators Einstein, Galileo, and Edison, it is clear that Einstein engaged in mostly theoretical innovation, Edison innovated practical or business solutions, and Galileo did a combination of the two. As I mentioned earlier, Einstein's work was more fundamental in nature, while Edison's work was more tangible, and Einstein conducted mostly thought experiments (e.g., riding the light wave), while Edison conducted experiments in his laboratory. Looking at various activity-based innovations, we can classify them into the four categories discussed in chapter 3—fundamental, platform, derivative, and variation—based on the amount of effort and the speed-of-thought components (knowledge, play, and imagination).

Various types of innovations are developed by differing degrees of speed of thought. A fundamental innovation may require a more meditative process, allowing one to think of theories, concepts, or solutions without significant physical experimentation. In fundamental innovation, knowledge and imagination are key components (e.g., Einstein's thought experiments). A platform innovation involves relatively less knowledge and imagination, but rather more play and experimentation. A variation innovation requires more play than does a fundamental innovation. As mentioned earlier, fundamental innovations can take much longer to develop than the other innovation types; as a result, more variation and platform innovations will result than fundamental ones.

Scouting for Innovation

A business must be fully aware of its surrounding environment and its own ecosystem in order to identify opportunities for innovation. It must not only complete competitive benchmarking, but also look for customer pain, inconvenience, conflicting design situations, and implicit or explicit demand for new capabilities. Maximizing the use of a company's existing products or services by making them more convenient, less costly, and more fun is a simple beginning for creating innovation opportunities.

Innovation is sometimes thought of as glamorous—looking for the "next big thing." But it breaks down into determining what the next big thing is, what it takes to produce it, and how to make it a success. In order to expand into future products, a company must first learn the historical trends and evolutions of similar products. Performing regression analysis, accelerating the evolving trend, and expanding the horizon can help identify new opportunities for breakthrough innovation.

TIME TO INNOVATION	SCOPE OF INNOVATION	ESTIMATED HEAD COUNTS	RESOURCES REQUIRED
This moment to days	Variation	Individuals	Experiments Trial & Error Tools
Days to weeks	Derivative	Small Group (10s)	Knowledge, thinking, simulations, computers
Weeks to months	Platform	Large Group (100s)	Expertise Deep thinking Larger experiments Larger computers
Months to years	Fundamental	Larger Group (1000s)	Experts Dedicated thinkers Super-computers Theorists

FIGURE 4.1 Resource Planning and Feasibility Analysis

Besides extending and exploring, enlisting established networks can create the potential for new innovation. Figure 4.1 serves as a guide for feasibility analysis and resource planning (the present) to develop innovative solutions (the future).

Analyzing opportunities to innovate helps a business recognize, prioritize, and maximize return on investment. This analysis also helps to define innovation targets in terms of performance, value, price, cost, resources, and time.

Avoiding Innovation Failures

We all understand that ideas are a dime a dozen. No shortage of ideas exists. Breakthrough innovations need a large number of ideas. A culture of continual innovation therefore must be created in which ideas are routinely sought and managed.

The most important aspect of making innovative products is to avoid failures caused by three factors:

1. An inability to introduce the innovation to potential users (i.e., the marketing plan),

2. Poor optimization of design for reproducibility, and

3. An insufficient value proposition to change behaviors due to a lack of sufficient innovation.

These failure modes can be avoided by:

1. Developing a commercialization plan (a plan developed with the support of required resources),

2. Planning operations for reproducibility (designed to virtually perfect the solution), and

3. Demonstrating the extent of the innovation (researched and purposefully imagined)

Establishing Innovation Projects

Once the opportunities are identified, analyzed, enhanced, and sifted through success filters, potential projects must be defined for new innovative product development. To prevent project delays, a company must deploy a process for innovation that in some way includes the following five steps: target, explore, develop, optimize, and commercialize (TEDOC). The commercialization must be a distinct and required phase, as it is the divider between success and failure (i.e., innovation and creativity).

To some extent, everyone is creative and innovative; but when people are asked to be "innovative," they find it is not easy to produce results. TEDOC represents the key aspects of successful innovation that one must be aware of for developing skills and competency in innovating on demand for breakthrough solutions.

The TEDOC Methodology

Target—A clear need for innovation based on opportunity analysis

Explore—Research, benchmark, and analyze the opportunity, and gain expertise knowledge in the domain

Develop—Alternative innovative breakthrough solutions to maximize innovative components

Optimize—The final solution for minimal diversion in operations and delivery

Commercialize—Rapid access to the marketplace and customers to ensure premium margins and above market return on investment

TARGET

Defining an opportunity for innovation is critical. In order to develop breakthrough innovations, a business needs to know what to innovate. To determine what to innovate, they must look at existing needs. These needs are found in complaints, nagging or chronic problems, indecision, frustrations, technical limitations, circumstances, and competitors' organizational limitations. A business should also look at the maturity of its industry, trends in supplier performance, SWOT (Strengths, Weaknesses, Opportunities, Threats) analyses, industry performance, and the available market.

Once potential innovation opportunities are identified, the innovation team must document the key benefits of the solution to be innovated and determine the key measures of its success.

EXPLORE

A company needs to fully and quickly research its opportunities to beef up its necessary competencies. The innovation team should identify and research keywords associated with the opportunity for innovation, generate new ideas, answer questions, discover new questions, and produce more new ideas. These ideas then need to be combined, filtered, analyzed, and prioritized. They are analyzed as input to the solution to be developed. Then, the team experiments with them to find solutions. Tools in this phase may include creativity, research, brainstorming, affinity diagrams, failure mode and effects analysis (FMEA), and process thinking.

DEVELOP

Innovators need to develop alternate solutions that are significantly innovative. Experience shows that following the "rule of two" (discussed in chapter 1) helps stretch imaginations as people experiment. According to the rule of two, in order for a solution to be a breakthrough innovation, it must affect the performance of the desired features by a factor of two (dividing or multiplying). In other words, if less is better, halve (divide by two) it, and if more is better, then double (multiply by two) it. The change is expected to force a different approach to the current position.

The extent of innovation depends upon the innovation team's efforts (the amount of available time committed to the desired innovation), knowledge (domain expertise), ability to play (experimentation), and overall imagination (extrapolation to achieve breakthrough innovation). In order to create a unique selling proposition and overcome barriers or competition, a company must try to maximize innovation rather than just create a minimal innovation. Tools used in this phase include the competency necessary to create new knowledge, creativity for proposing alternative solutions, evaluation and analytical methods, and the facility to conduct experiments.

OPTIMIZE

Many great innovations remain marginally successful and have limited shelf life because they are not effectively and economically reproducible. A great design alone does not provide a good return on innovation. The optimize phase focuses on maximizing the economic benefit of the innovation. In the current R&D-driven product development environment, the optimize phase is the most significant step missing for ensuring a product's success. Due to a lack of optimization in the design or preproduction stage(s), manufacturing operations suffer from design constraints. Today, most designs are quickly verified for their functionality and performance, but only on a limited sample size of potential process conditions during a product's life cycle. The prototype or pilot run that appears acceptable may actually result in continual rework and field failures leading to a significant adverse impact on profit margins. The tools typically used in this stage are process management, optimization software programs, and the facility to conduct the necessary experiments.

COMMERCIALIZE

Many entrepreneurs and innovators fail in this phase—an innovative solution exists, but not enough people who would value it know about it. Without development, there is no creativity; without optimization, there is no profit; and without commercialization, there is no innovation. The commercialization of a solution converts creativity into innovation. Every innovator, therefore, must learn the process of commercialization and develop the knowledge necessary to create value. In the commercialization phase, an innovation team must practice strategic thinking about methods of pricing a solution, messages of value proposition, viral marketing, business planning, and making deals for licensing or selling the breakthrough solutions.

Leadership guru Steven Covey says to begin a task with the end in mind. In the case of innovation, begin innovating with commercialization in mind. Often, commercializing is tougher than discovering the innovative product. The full cycle of innovation starts with the identification of the need for an innovative solution and ends with the commercialization of the innovative solution.

Developing the ability to innovate on demand makes the task of commercialization easier, as the innovative solution has already been sold. However, improvement in the success rate of demand-driven innovation depends on the speed of the innovation. Once a company masters the process of innovation through practice and commitment, it can innovate quickly.

However, after a company has invested in deploying innovation through cultural transformation, it must take steps to sustain the culture of innovation. Every company should begin its innovation journey with the end in mind; in this case, an effort to sustain innovation must be carefully planned and practiced to perpetuate the culture of accelerated introduction of new products or solutions.

Seven Killers of Innovation

Corporate leadership understands innovation is important for success; employees understand how to innovate; and innovation occurs in every business. However, the extent and rate of innovation have been insufficient. Following are seven killers of innovation. These factors are known to suppress our creative instincts:

1. Harmful Language—Phrases such as *used to, hate it, shut up,* and *why* have been used on people since their childhoods to discourage innovative thinking. *Used to* implies resistance to change; *hate it* is used to demoralize a person; *shut up* is a personal attack on the innovator; and *why* can be used to discourage the innovator from trying something new.

2. Standardized Tests—SAT- and ACT-like standard tests promote rote test-taking skills and do not test for or encourage true learning. Individuals conforming to the norms succeed and have no reason to be innovative.

3. College Education and Grading System—Many college courses are taught to a crowd with little student-instructor or student-student interaction, require standard assignments, and promote regurgitation of outdated material. These students are then graded according to their test-taking skills. Such grading practices may make teaching easier, but they limit learning. Teaching without grading results in learning is a prerequisite for innovation.

4. Group Thinking—Studies have shown that conventional group thinking methods are not suitable for innovation. Experience indicates that in a typical brainstorming session, only about 20 to 30 percent of attendees participate actively, while the remaining 70

to 80 percent remain passive. Instead of group thinking and fragmented execution, innovation requires grouped individual-innovative-thinking and networked execution.

5. Subject Expertise—Mastery of a subject poses a dilemma. On the one hand, domain expertise is a necessary requirement for innovation; on the other hand, expertise has an adverse impact because of associated baggage—Trust me, I know!

6. Excessive Focus—Similar to expertise, too much focus on one thing can limit free or diverse thinking and experience and inhibit innovative thinking.

7. Overly Busy Employees—Most companies hire the best and brightest—and give them little time to think. The highly qualified employees are kept busy fighting fires generated by rushed management decisions, such as the launch of new products or shipment of products in an unrealistic time frame.

Accelerating Innovation

In the technology age, information is a commodity, and intelligence is a competitive advantage. Mining information to extract unique intelligence and create new knowledge must become routine. Continual analysis and interpretation of market, process, product, and business information are necessary to identify new areas of revenue growth and innovation. Corporate leadership must develop plans to introduce innovative products, services, or solutions to achieve profit margin and revenue growth. Expectations for the introduction of new products, solutions, and services help create a schedule for efficient and predictable innovation. Adherence to such a schedule requires a process that works for the organization and encompasses the following: inspiring leadership, a culture of creativity, idea management, engineering skills, optimization tools, operations capability, marketing resources, and an economic mind-set.

Every organization is innovative to a certain extent. The challenge, however, is to innovate better and faster. Accelerating innovation requires formalizing and optimizing the innovation process, which can only be accomplished by understanding its components, committing resources to the various types of innovations, and driving the success of the innovation process. Leadership must not question whether innovation works; it must instead challenge the organization's members to innovate more.

Consider a hypothetical path leading to the development of the iPod. Personal computers were developed in the early eighties. New peripheral or derivative technologies were then developed, and new capabilities were added to the computer, including audio. Concurrently, in the music industry, the Discman was the latest and greatest discovery of its era, but stagnation had crept into personal music devices. MP3 technology arose, and devices representing the trends in the personal music arena developed. Conflicts soon arose. Some opportunists observed the market, thought about their products and the computer, and saw the potential for disruption. Why not strip the computer of everything except the music and significantly reduce its size?

Next, commercialization issues were evaluated, new distribution methods were developed, and finally, the solution was refined before the iPod took over the marketplace. To develop devices with iPod-like success, corporate leadership must relentlessly pursue innovation in their companies and continually look for new opportunities. A "big" opportunity can only be realized when working on many smaller opportunities. The incrementally innovative new products will help revenue grow gradually until a major breakthrough occurs and a new revenue plateau is established.

Chapter Five

Innovation Execution

Innovation is a necessity to maintain a competitive edge. Customers are becoming more demanding and restless. They want unique products, and they will not wait for them. In response to this demand, companies like Nokia, Sony, IBM, Apple, 3M, and Proctor & Gamble have been innovating for a long time. Some companies promote innovation by allowing employees to spend 15 percent of their time on independent projects. They may also buy innovation or collaborate for innovation. Historically speaking, most innovation is a function of research and development (R&D) departments. Businesses today recognize that they must learn a new process for innovation in order to practice and produce more of it.

According to a survey conducted by Emily Chasan (2006), corporate leadership struggles to raise the profile of innovation in their companies because of internal barriers, such as culture and climate. Yet corporate leaders are looking to innovate in their business models to drive growth. About one in seven of the participating CEOs thinks internal R&D is a good source for innovation. Moreover, many CEOs are unwilling to make innovation their top priority because of their lack of understanding of the innovation process, and only one in five executives in the United States and India want to take ownership of innovation. These leaders realize measures used today of innovation do not strongly correlate with the top or the bottom line.

At an international symposium on innovation methodologies (Eurescom 2002), the main challenges appeared to be the lack of knowledge of innovation techniques and the lack of sharing of innovation results. To overcome these challenges, the suggestion was made to establish a "European Innovation Award" and create an innovation toolbox for accessing innovation knowledge.

A review of the literature and other various sources shows that as many innovation methodologies exist as the number of users or organizations. Since many people consider innovation an art, every innovator or innovating organization develops a unique approach to the process. Most approaches appear to have common elements; however, the details of the process and an understanding of its components are lacking. Currently, a strong correlation between types of methodologies and their performance has not been established. The questions then remain: Which innovation approach is a good methodology? What should the criteria be to evaluate a methodology of innovation?

In order for us to be able to evaluate a methodology, it must support some theoretical objectives, some basic tenets must form its foundation, and relevant measures must be present to monitor and improve the innovation process in terms of efficiency and outcome. In other words, a repeatable and continuously improving system must be in place, allowing for the standardization of structure and discipline for the innovation process. Such a system must require that it be taught to others, so that everyone clearly understands the innovation methodology.

The breakthrough innovation methodology was formulated based on implementation of its elements at various businesses and the logical understanding of innovation activities. As explained in chapter 3, Brinnovation bases its tenets on the following assumptions:

1. Innovation and creativity are the same when produced in real time on demand;

2. Innovative solutions can be generated on demand in a knowledge economy;

3. The building block of innovation is a "networked individual;" and

4. Innovation is a function of speed of thought.

Every individual or group of individuals is fundamentally a creative entity because of the colossal capability of the human brain. No two tasks accomplished by any one person are identical. The ability to develop a creative solution on demand is an innovation, as it is bound to create value. Instead of developing a solution and then commercializing it, innovation on demand implies identifying an opportunity first and then inventing a solution for that problem. A group of individuals thinking independently and working together is more effective than a group of people brainstorming (thinking together) and working independently. Therefore, a cluster of people by itself does not become more innovative; instead, a network of thinking individuals is more innovative. Such a network enables individuals to learn quickly, think independently, collaborate virtually, and innovate when needed.

For individuals to become active thinkers, they need to have broader experience and must be able to practice combinatorial thought experiments. Since the possible combinatorial thought experiments could be numerous, an active thinker needs to be able to think fast. The speed of thought matters and is affected by knowledge, which allows us to develop shortcuts to prioritizing information and conduct thought experiments faster.

Thinking and conducting thought experiments take time. They require motivation, stamina, and a rested mind. With this understanding, corporations must create an environment in which people can think freely. One of the main inhibitors to thinking freely is fear, which executives must try to drive out of their organizations. Driving out fear, however, does not mean removing accountability for actions or consequences.

Many businesses begin when a person with an innovative idea takes action to realize it. Diversification of the business helps promote growth. Businesses experience many up-and-down performance cycles, including cycles of loss and profit, growth and downsizing, and mergers and acquisitions. Through these cycles, businesses go through many changes, which can lead them to profitable growth or a hard landing. The hard landing can be attributed to the management style, unexpected market erosion, loss of a major customer, externally funded growth, or simply a lot of waste because of poor management of resources. Profitable growth, on the other hand, requires innovative strategies and solutions.

The earlier model of R&D-driven product or service development cannot keep up with market demand for innovative solutions. Global connectivity, knowledge sharing, trade, and opportunities have changed the former business model; the current business model involves global customers, global development, and global innovation. Innovative thinking and activity based on innovation must become routine. The marketplace now expects employees to produce innovative output on demand, with value and on time. The time of innovation can be from real time to years. The innovations can range from a simple variation to a fundamental discovery of a new phenomenon.

In today's knowledge economy, business orientation is shifting from manufacturing to service. Businesses, whether manufacturing or service, gear themselves toward managing intangibles more than managing widgets. More important, the intangibles include knowledge management and innovation. In a conventional business model, innovation is a function within the R&D community. However, the role of innovation has changed in today's knowledge economy. Experience shows that now everyone's job is to innovate at relevant levels in an organization. In today's environment, innovation is a tool for creating the unique selling proposition (USP). Innovation is driving the competitive bar to higher levels.

Encouraging Innovation in the Organization

To achieve higher performance continually, business leadership must be cognizant of the intellectual potential of employees. Committing to innovation throughout the organization will accelerate its performance, as employees collaborate with executives rather than resist innovation. Such organizational interaction reduces friction among employees and managers, reveals new opportunities for innovation, reduces costs, and creates a sense of ownership among employees.

Commitment to continual innovation requires a good understanding of the theory, practice, and results of innovation methods. Scattered and successful application of innovation methods demonstrates that the innovation process is more than random creativity. Like any process, one can benchmark the best innovators and organizations to learn and innovate. Einstein is recognized as the best thinker, while Edison the best innovator. Einstein's discoveries are more fundamental, while Edison's work was more product-based innovation.

How did Edison innovate so frequently? He understood the innovation process, built his laboratory in Menlo Park, New Jersey, and guided his researchers to produce solutions on demand. He built factories and products based on his innovations and accelerated that growth in wartime. Edison was not acting as an innovative person; instead, he was seeking opportunities and producing innovative solutions. He expanded his knowledge, changed his expertise from one field to the other, and innovated on demand.

To institutionalize innovation on demand, benchmarking against Einstein and Edison is important. Einstein mastered thought experiments and saw something in nothing, while Edison perfected product innovation to produce innovative solutions on demand, as evidenced by the number of patents (over one thousand) assigned to him. The corporate process for breakthrough innovation must consider the following aspects.

Defining Innovation

Clayton M. Christensen and Michael R. Raynor, in their book, *The Innovator's Solution*, emphasize sustained innovation in achieving corporate business growth. A successful era of superior performance in the life of a corporation occurs because of some innovative disruption. Sustaining innovation requires not just the ideas, but also the packaging of ideas for growth opportunities. Even Six Sigma emphasizes breakthrough improvement; the methods to produce breakthrough solutions were not developed.

Innovation is often defined as open-ended. Everyone has a different perception of innovation and creativity. The extent of innovation can be incremental (implying a little change), radical (representing a disruptive change), or of a general purpose (implying a new discovery). One way to define innovation is "doing differently." The question, then, is how much change should the innovation create? Considering the process of evaluating change, a change is statistically significant when it exceeds at least 47.5 percent in the desired characteristics. The 47.5 percent change corresponds to two standard deviations from the current process' typical performance as shown in figure 5.1. When the change in a parameter is statistically significant, the probability of occurrence is small, but the change is a breakthrough innovation. Thus, innovation happens when an activity is carried out differently in order to create value through products, services, or solutions.

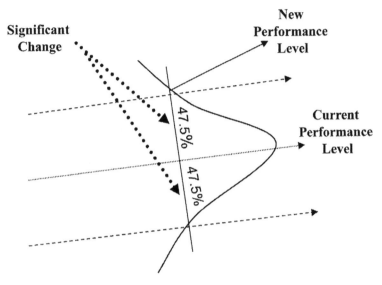

FIGURE 5.1 Breakingthrough Solutions

Innovation happens daily, whether it is a simple container by Rubbermaid; an Apple iPod; Panasonic's robust laptop; a cell phone from Motorola, Sony, LG, or Nokia; a grill from Weber; new drugs from a pharmaceutical company; or a printer from HP, Canon, or Xerox. Many companies are serially innovative, while others are sporadically innovative. Thus, innovation is not a new thing, but it is not often systematic. In order to accelerate and sustain innovation to meet continual demand for new products, services, or solutions, corporations must deliberately recognize organizational needs and address them. This recognition requires an understanding of strengths and weaknesses, company leadership for innovation, and a clear link between innovation and the corporate values and organizational strategy.

In order to understand an organization's strengths and weaknesses, leaders must conduct an assessment using simple tools like a checklist, survey, or performance analysis. A thorough analysis must include the social, operational, financial, customer, and leadership aspects of the organization. The social aspects may be comprised of corporate values, teamwork, and employee participation. The operational assessment includes an emphasis on creativity in process management and daily activities, the ability to take risks, and a general decision-making approach. The financial aspects are resources committed to innovation-related activities, training, rewards, and revenue generated from innovative solutions. The leadership aspects are creativity at the leadership level, inclination for risks, recognition for success, understanding for genuine innovation failures, and keen participation in innovation. The assessment's objective is to show how an organization can transform into an agile and thinking one. A thinking organization is one that promotes learning new skills, experiencing new domains, and productively applying lessons learned for developing innovative solutions.

In a training session, people are always looking for a trick, a case study, software, or a formula to apply quickly so they can reject the tool for its differences and application difficulty. Quickly applied methods, however, are not adequately developed and will not produce the desired results. This rote application of a technique is called reproductive thinking. Accordingly, if everyone learns a technique to design a product and applies it the same way, the expected result will also be the same.

Every problem and every company are different. Thus, the application of a technique must be adapted creatively to the opportunity under consideration. Figure 5.2 illustrates how a problem can be solved just by doing something and how many impractical creative ideas can help to solve the problem. "Just doing something" to solve a problem often leads to new problems, though; while in the case of using "imaginative ideas," nothing really happens. Thus, the solution needed for the problem often lies in the application of creative ideas.

One of the challenges in a corporation is to allow time for thinking. As mentioned earlier, companies often hire smart people, keep them busy in fighting fires, and give them no time to think. The 3M Company allows employees to spend 15 percent of their work time as they wish thinking of something new, learning something new, or doing whatever they like. In order to justify time for thinking, or the investment in innovation, systems thinking as shown in figure 5.3 must be occurring.

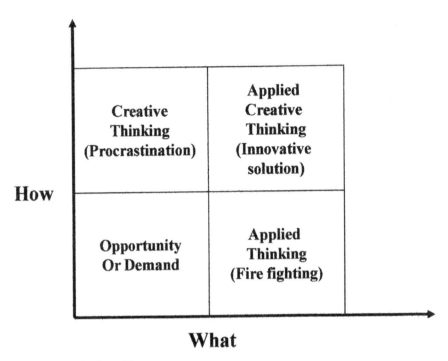

FIGURE 5.2 Thinking Types

As the figure shows, innovating a solution for an opportunity at a level higher than the level of its symptoms is essential. For example, if a department is having a problem at one network node, the innovative solution should be implemented above that node level (i.e., at the server), so all nodes can benefit from it. Similarly, if an opportunity is identified for an innovative solution, the opportunity must be defined at a higher level. This elevation of the opportunity creates more value, due to its expanded scope of application, and justifies resources for developing the innovative solution. Once the solution is developed, it can then be applied to specific situations.

Systems Thinking requires that the corporate leadership practice process thinking, establish measurements for monitoring performance, and promote risk-taking in developing innovative solutions. In today's economy, the global diffusion of opportunities mandates that every society continually innovate in its domain of expertise in order to create value. Otherwise, by the law of diffusion, migration of opportunities from higher-cost to lower-cost locations will cause societal frustration.

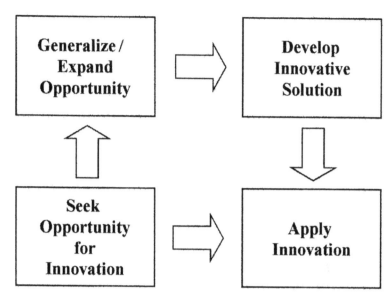

FIGURE 5.3 Systems Thinking

To maintain market leadership, a company must launch a multi-pronged approach to grow the top line as well as the bottom line. Many improvement efforts to perfect the bottom line eventually lead to a business downsizing because of a lack of sales. Businesses must develop new products, services, and solutions. The demand for innovative products or solutions has become a norm. Committing to continual innovation requires a good understanding of theory, practice, and the results of the innovation methods. The widespread and successful application of innovation clearly indicates that the innovation process is more than random creativity.

An organization attempting to institutionalize innovation must determine its methodology of choice. There are as many innovation methodologies out there as there are innovation consultants. Therefore, the reasons for selecting one must be based on a deep understanding of the innovation process. Some methodologies are measurement heavy, which leads to a number-driven innovation approach without a predictable outcome. A successful innovation methodology must incorporate inspiration from leadership, involvement of employees, and outcomes for higher value. Such methodology will include planning, organization, a process, tools, measurements, collaboration, and celebration.

Building an Innovative Organization

PLANNING

The exact method to implement innovation processes to produce on-demand innovation is still not well known. Successful implementation requires understanding the innovation process well enough to teach others and multiply resources. The list of challenges in institutionalizing innovation can be extensive. Some of the common issues are the following:

- Too much focus on the bottom line and cost reduction

- Wrong measurements of good performance; for example, head-count reduction is a measure of lean implementation (an improvement methodology)

- Lack of focus on revenue growth through innovative products, services, and solutions

- Lack of strategic intent to institutionalize innovation

- Inadequate understanding of the innovation process

- Fear of failure and punishment

- No time for or expectation of the intellectual involvement of employees

- Insufficient incentives and rewards directly linked to innovation

- Poorly performing systems used to test new things effectively

Considering the issues associated with the lack of innovative practices in corporations, it is obvious that a different approach must be taken to plan for institutionalizing innovation. With a clear commitment to innovate new processes, products, or solutions, the corporate leadership must develop a strategic plan. In order to approach innovation as a scientific process, this strategic plan must address the following:

- Strategic commitment

- Organizational alignment

- Measures of innovation

- Plan for innovation
  - Culture of creativity
  - Innovation room
  - Establishment of innovation-friendly policies
  - Communication of innovation
  - Incentives for innovation
  - Demand for innovation
  - Innovation training and certification
  - Excellence in the idea-management process
  - Innovation management
  - Rapid commercialization of innovation
- Return on investment (ROI) in innovation management
- Strategic adjustment

LEADERSHIP FOR INNOVATION

Successful leaders recognize the significance of innovation and the leadership needed. The leader must believe in and understand the role an innovative culture can play in the growth of a corporation in the future. Such leaders consider innovation in all areas of business and create a culture of innovation. To lead an organization toward becoming a learning and innovating entity, the organizational environment must influence thoughts, planning, and acts. For example, Johnson Controls, an organization that has lasted over a century, recognizes the role of innovation (as stated in its values) as responding to its customers' needs through improvement and creation of new and better products.

To launch or sustain the innovation initiative, the leader must commit to recognizing the intellectual involvement of all employees, valuing all information available, and appreciating the evolution of all employees and processes. The leader of an organization sets beliefs, initiatives, and the environment for innovation. A visionary leadership develops both a corporate meaning of innovation in the organizational context as well as a corporate strategy for learning and innovating success. The leadership establishes expectations and recognition of innovations by employees at all levels. The strategy involves training; recognition; innovation expectations and objectives; the roles of executives, managers, and employees; intellectual property aspects; and the transformation from innovation to commercialization of the product or service to realize economic benefits. Executives and managers can set an example through their own behaviors, attitudes, innovative thinking, actions, and support of innovation.

Organizational Structure for Innovation

In order to promote innovation and integrate it into normal daily activities, the organization must create an innovation model and allocate the resources to make it work. In other words, innovation must become an element of business profitability and growth streams. Innovation begins with ideas, so a mechanism to generate ideas from all employees of the company must be in place. The next step is to provide the structure for reviewing the ideas for their relevance and applicability. Each idea must receive supportive feedback. Employees must be encouraged to think and reflect on their experiences and look to the future for new ideas and innovative products, services, or solutions. Innovative or learning organizations support some kind of in-house library, where employees can browse through learning resources to reenergize themselves intellectually.

A recommended organizational structure can incorporate the elements shown in figure 5.4, which illustrates that the culture of creativity cultivates ideas—ideas that become innovations, which can be transformed into products or services for economic gain. Though developing such an organizational structure only makes sense, many organizations lack this formal structure to establish a culture of creativity, idea management, and innovation leadership.

Culture of Innovation

A culture of innovation begins with an awareness of the organizational commitment to innovation and a visible room for innovation, as shown

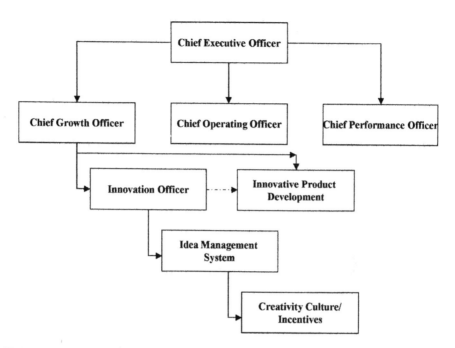

FIGURE 5.4 Organization for Innovation

in figure 5.5. A typical layout for a home includes a variety of rooms, such as a study room, a kitchen, bedrooms, bathrooms, a living room, a family room, and a den for relevant routine activities. A kitchen gives people ideas about food. A study room stimulates ideas about the topic of study in mind. Similarly, if an organization wants to have ideas from its employees, it needs to create the environment, even a room, for creative ideas.

The environment must be one that provides an appropriate sensory experience and resources for knowledge in the field of interest. The leadership wants employees to develop observation-fueled insights, a keen eye for details, and inspiration to find ways to do things differently. The objective is to innovate on demand with purposeful effort. In my analysis of the innovation process and its impact on the brain, I have found the following conditions must exist for an organization to become innovative:

1. A comfortable environment for absorbing information

2. Effective incentives for learning and comprehension.

3. Employees with good time management and healthy practices

4. Inspiration for new knowledge experimentation.

5. A place to rest and time for reflection.

6. Corporate values and decision making to support innovation among employees.

Innovation requires work. People are innovative in their domain of expertise. Innovation does create economic or social value. It occurs as a result of determined, focused, and deliberate work demanding persistence, diligence, and commitment.

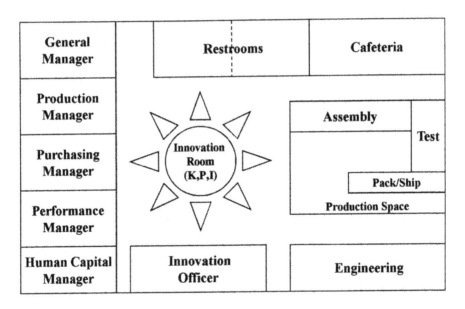

FIGURE 5.5 Room for Innovation

Process for Innovation

A business is a collection of processes, including the innovation process. Therefore, applying the principles of process management (the 4Ps—prepare, perform, perfect, and progress), as shown in figure 5.6, to the innovation process helps us to understand the components of innovation. Like any other process, the innovation process requires input in terms of tools, information, materials, methods, and skilled people. Creatively and comprehensively identifying inputs is important for innovations.

Loosely defining the method of innovation allows for maximum human creativity. The flexibility to learn, experiment, fail, and innovate within some defined framework is essential. The innovation process must include people experiencing a variety of things outside their norm or regular domain of work. This will allow them to create combinations or associations and validate outcomes.

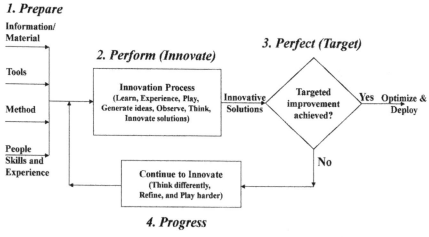

FIGURE 5.6 Process for Innovation

The mental massage of various concepts or models results in practical ideas that can help in formulating products, processes, or services. Ultimately, every employee has the responsibility to play and create value through innovation.

If the innovation turns out to be impractical or too costly for further implementation, the originator of that innovation must not become dejected or disappointed. The creative or innovation process itself should be a lot of fun (rather than people waiting to have fun with the resulting product). Generating one truly innovative product or service requires many ideas. Therefore, creative play is a necessity, idea generation is imperative, and engaging in innovation is every employee's overriding responsibility to him- or herself, the organization, and society. Even if ideas do not turn into products or services, people need to continue to play. The persistence and perseverance will eventually lead to innovation on demand.

Measuring Innovation

Because innovation is a loosely defined process, it is difficult to measure. Innovation is often measured in terms of ideas generated, patents filed, engineering awards given, new products introduced, revenue from new products earned, number of people deployed in innovation, or hours allocated for innovation. To be effective, the measurements must be established as needed by the particular organization. The intent of measurements must be to assess the role of innovation in the growth of a corporation. The Six Sigma Business Scorecard identifies a set of measurements relating to growth and profitability. Innovation is a critical aspect of the Six Sigma Business Scorecard. The ten measurements utilized in determining the business performance index (BPIn) are as follows:

1. Employee recognition by CEO

2. Profitability

3. Rate of improvement

4. Employee recommendations

5. Purchase ($) / Sales ($) ratio

6. Suppliers' quality

7. Operational Sigma

8. Timeliness

9. New business / Sales ratio

10. Customer satisfaction

Measurements 1, 4, and 9 relate to innovation in the organization. The CEO recognizes an employee based on innovative solutions with a significant and visible impact on corporate performance. Employee recommendations measure the intellectual engagement of the employees, and new business measures the financial outcome of the innovative product or service. A combination of three measurements can create an initial innovation index that has a significantly positive impact on the corporate performance.

Training Employees in Innovation

Any major corporate transformation has to begin with education to ensure learning, consistency, productivity, and results. The objective of training is to help people become familiar with the innovation process, accentuate their capabilities, and direct their creativity in the direction of corporate goals. Innovation training should include an understanding of the aspects of innovation and require employees to become familiar with its components (i.e., knowledge, play, and imagination).

The training for innovation should include hands-on experience in researching and playing with combinations of components of the innovative solution and exposure to an environment for imagining new solutions. The training may consist of getting people into a planned environment, giving them the learning objectives, and turning them loose. Irrespective of the method of innovation training, the corporation must set goals for innovation training and measure the training effectiveness in terms of the number of innovations, the extent of innovation, and the financial impact.

Recognition and Rewards

Whether innovation initiatives will be sustained depends on the continual success of the activities, excitement about doing the innovative work, and the inclusion of everyone. As expectations for innovation in various functions are established, the leadership must verify performance against the expectations and make appropriate adjustments. If an organization commits to innovation as a key component of its business strategy, it must ensure that various phases of the innovation process are executed with excellence.

In order to promote innovation, recognizing innovation successes is critical. Publicizing success is as important as understanding the failures. In a corporation, when creativity, innovation, and risk-taking become basic principles, measures must exist to recognize and reward innovators. Recognition can be as simple as a "thank-you" note, some public recognition at a banquet, or an announcement in the local newspaper. Each success is recognized differently—sometimes with financial incentives and other times with personal notes.

Irrespective of the value or type of recognition, recognizing a specific act or outcome of creativity or innovation is essential. It can be at any level—the idea level, solution level, or field-performance level. Incentives should be given for submitting an idea about process or product improvement, writing and publishing a paper in a magazine or journal, obtaining a patent, successfully completing the evaluation of a new product or concept, providing new ideas about daily activities, engaging in a superior act of engineering, or transforming an innovation into a commercial product or service. Ultimately, innovation must be an empowering, rewarding, and enriching experience for everyone involved.

Launching an Innovation Initiative

Innovation begins with the intellectual involvement of employees through their ideas. The process of getting employee suggestions, ideas, or recommendations has been in existence for a long time. However, its effective implementation and success rates are far from satisfactory for many reasons, including the lack of understanding of value and importance of innovation to corporate growth and profitability and lack of an established process for idea management.

Just like purchasing, sales, production, or quality processes, innovation must become a standard process in a corporation. First leadership must be committed in order for the implementation of the innovation process to be successful. Next, an innovation policy must be defined, expectations established, resources allocated, and measurements to monitor innovation value put in place. Then, innovation should be incorporated into business planning and budgeting activities in order for it to become visible on the management radar.

The first step in creating innovative thinking in an organization is to establish a good idea-management program. A high-quality idea-management program creates a long-lasting, positive impression on employees because of its sincerity, regular follow-up, and achievement recognition. The purpose, scope, responsibility, ownership, tools, and procedures for the idea-management process also need to be established. In this way, the method for handling unacceptable or not-so-good ideas can be clearly defined and documented, and the conversion of good ideas into viable economic value will be a realistic goal. This must be accomplished through training, communication, and other business processes. An idea program is not about complaints, criticism of management, or getting even with workplace enemies. Idea management is all about contributing to employees' success by achieving improvement.

Every employee in a corporation is capable of being innovative. Everyone has pride for something he or she has accomplished. Bringing out each person's ability to achieve significant improvement requires an expectation, which leadership must establish and strive to implement. The intellectual participation of employees must become the leadership's mantra. All successful leaders see potential in their employees and exploit it to achieve sustained improvement.

Chapter Six

Managing Innovation

Practicing innovation is an explicitly strategic initiative for some companies, while for others, this practice is an implicit one. The challenge to a strategy for innovation arises from a lack of understanding of the process. Once the process is understood, as described in earlier chapters, it becomes possible to precisely strategize and plan for its execution.

The performance of the innovation strategy can be both assessed by using measurements across the supply chain and accelerated based on opportunities for improvement in the supply chain. Up to this point, innovation has been an inefficient R&D activity with unmeasured performance and unpredictable outcomes (and even a negative correlation with its input or resources). With a clearly defined framework in terms of resources, knowledge, play, and imagination, leaders can define the innovation process, establish a strategy for growth through new products and services with a certain confidence, and measure the process's success.

In order to launch the innovation initiative, the map of innovation must be understood and adopted. Figure 6.1, "Innovation Map," shows that innovation starts at the top, where the leader commits to sustained profitable growth rather than just "making money." Growth-driven leaders are interested in innovation. Organizations can realize sustained growth if they create a growth office, which is headed by an innovation leader. This office's purpose is to ensure continual growth through innovation.

Once the responsibility for innovation has been clearly assigned, a good understanding of the innovation process will help in making progress. Again, the four components of a good innovation process are resources, knowledge, play, and imagination. Without resources, innovation is not possible. Innovation does require investment of financial and intellectual resources. Once the resources are deployed, ideas for innovation are managed and commercialized as necessary to achieve a significant return on that investment. The process continues from commercialization back to concepts to sustain and accelerate innovation.

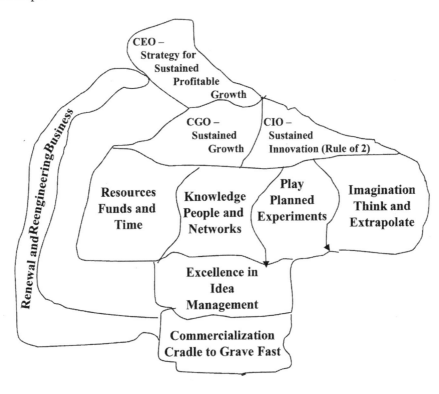

FIGURE 6.1 Innovation Map

Resources for Innovation

Allocating the resources to support the commitment to innovation is a critical first action if an organization wants to execute the strategy well. Resources can either be financial or human capital. Proper utilization of human capital offers many opportunities for accelerating the innovation of new products and services. Of course, the human capital is an outcome of the financial investment in employees. In order to grow human capital, a corporation must develop tactics to invest in employees through training and exposure to experiences in various aspects of business.

Human capital consisting of intellectual capability is one of the most underutilized resources. Since so much opportunity exists, any improvement in its usage will have a significant impact on the outcome. If the human brain's average utilization doubled from about 5 percent to 10 percent, the world would be a very different place. In such a scenario, a continual stream of new products or services would result. Innovation on demand and mass customization for customers would become the new status quo. When the switch is made from utilizing primarily mechanical resources to utilizing primarily intellectual ones, nothing is standard anymore; that is the impact of such a change.

Financial capital still plays a role in providing support to the innovation strategy. Organizations must invest in facility and policy upgrades to create the appropriate ambiance for creativity, an innovation room or physical space for experiments, and enough time to reflect and dig deeper into available mental resources. Organizations like to hire best people in all functions and keep them busy running around. As a result, they do not feel comfortable sitting in their offices thinking because someone, including a supervisor, might think they are not doing any work. Managers love to see highly intelligent people run around, but rarely allow them time to use their brains.

One investment in innovation must be something similar to 3M's allowance of 15 percent time for thinking, creativity, or learning without any accountability. Setting up an innovation room is an additional investment that provides facilities and resources for accelerated learning, such as a library with research material, knowledge management software, a laboratory for experimentation, resources for benchmarking, and a solitary space for creative thinking without any distraction. Additional resources may be required for acquiring related new technology or tools to stretch organizational capability into new domains.

Organization Structure

Interestingly, every organization has a chief executive officer (CEO), chief operating officer (COO), and chief financial officer (CFO), or their equivalents. Some organizations have a chief technology officer (CTO) to lead new product development. Otherwise, most of the executives' attention is given to managing shareholders' perceptions of the organization as well as operational performance through cost reduction by pressuring suppliers and counting beans. Too much focus is on profit, and not enough is on growth. Money is spent in cutting costs—sometimes more than what is spent on developing new products and services. Employees' jobs, in the longer term, are dependent on developing future opportunities while still maintaining excellence in the portfolio.

In a typical R&D function, most of the resources are spent on development and little is spent on research. As a result, the product performance is marginal, and manufacturability is highly questionable. We quickly release new designs from the design engineering department to the product development department and wave good-bye. The manufacturing department pays for the questionable designs, which resulted from the lack of research and thoroughness in the design phase.

One of the reasons for marginal performance in manufacturing is the lack of defined targets for various parameters. Excellence in manufacturing is impossible without specifying targets. In the absence of targets, the product is built to specification limits and thus is produced with marginal performance.

Organizations must be realigned for innovation and excellence. Without excellence, innovations will be wasted in marginal performance environments. With excellence in operations, innovation can be accelerated because of faster and more precise feedback from experiments. To create a structure for launching and sustaining the innovation initiative, organizations must have an innovation officer or leader who can clearly bring economic sense to the design function and establish goals and processes to maximize the use of human capital.

All innovation begins with an idea in someone's mind; thus, excellence in idea management is a first and critical step to building an innovative organization. The management process must be standardized; every employee must contribute ideas to create value at the activity, process, or product level. One idea per quarter per employee is a reasonable starting goal upon which to build. Eventually, a continual flow of employee ideas toward development of new products or services in response to demand from customers or the marketplace should become the status quo.

Communicating the Innovation Message

Another important aspect in effectively executing the innovation strategy is the story. Leadership must develop a coherent message demonstrating the need for continual innovation, the benefits of innovation, and the consequences for not innovating enough to keep up with customer demand. Consistency and constancy of the message are critical in generating employee interest across the organization, minimizing conflicts, and aligning organizational resources toward the common goal. Typically, the story may include a finding from the benchmarking study identifying opportunities to gain market share and improve, or even create a message to achieve fundamental business objectives.

In many companies, the innovation message is subtle and conveyed through the actions of certain individuals in executive positions. For example, Steve Jobs at Apple drives and demands innovation. At Google, the work environment, also known as Googleplex, is committed to innovation and improving the "great" performance that promotes innovation there. Googleplex presents a unique lobby and hallway decor, office clusters, recreation spaces, a café, a snack room, and dogs to promote free thinking. All this is combined with the goal to develop innovative search-related products that promote continual innovation. The famous "15 percent investment in unaccountable time for employees to use" is a great way to communicate commitment to innovation.

Incentives and Controls

On a personal level, incentives have played a significant role in my desire to do things differently over the course of my career. The Silver Quill awards at Motorola, which are given for publishing articles, challenged me to write my first paper. Besides paying one hundred dollars per published page, the company also encouraged more writing by making the reward continual. In addition, filing any application for a patent at Motorola resulted in at least three hundred dollars in the early to mid-1980s, and the reward amount continued to grow as the application moved further down the patent filing process. In both cases, employees were rewarded for starting to do things differently.

Once people taste the flavor of doing things differently, it becomes difficult to stop. Understanding the innovation process in the brain shows that a personal incentive for learning can be much more effective than the simple incentive of achieving a more innovative outcome. Without learning multiple subjects, accelerating innovation is difficult. Thus, some incentives for learning must be put in place.

Interestingly, in tough times, learning incentives are the first to go at many companies, which only highlights operational problems leading to corporate troubles. Can you imagine turning around or growing a company without having education for employees and innovation in place? This scenario certainly sounds like a recipe for winding down business through continual cost-cutting and negative revenue growth.

Culture and Change

Culture and change are two nebulous aspects of a business. Culture is about how we interact with each other and how we make decisions. On a daily basis, these two factors depend on the corporation's values. Thus, defining the corporate values that can be withheld under dire circumstances is imperative. A methodology can become a strategy; a strategy can become the corporate values; and new values can become the culture. Thus, once the innovation strategy begins to be implemented, based on its success and widespread institutionalization, it can become a corporate value and result in employees at all levels doing things differently. Once everyone accepts and practices the value, they all simply do things differently. Thus, the innovation strategy can become part of the corporate culture.

One of the major topics within the realm of corporate leadership is "change." In one of his live seminars, Tom Peters asked a question, "How long does it take one person to change his mind?" He talked about managing resistance to change, how leadership gradually phases in new practices and implementation is fragmented because of resistance. Then, he answered his own question. He said the same people who resist at work actually change at home all the time when necessary. When people are doing things in a certain way and then are asked to change their behavior, resistance will occur because of the unanswered question, "Why should I change?"

People will change in no time if they know why they should adopt new practices and how they will benefit from the changes. To promote the change, leaders should make sure employees can see the benefits of innovation through incentives or recognition. In any case, the answer to Tom Peter's question is "a moment." Once the decision is made, change is made in the mind and the practice follows.

Figure 6.2, "The Innovation Thinking Matrix," shows various aspects of an organization that impact the mind of that organization once the decision is made to institutionalize innovation. As reported earlier, an individual can change his/her mind anytime; however, in a group of employees, different people choose different moments to make up their minds. If leadership communicates the strategy, employee roles, expected practices, and desired outcome, more employees will make the decision to accept the innovation initiative faster. Then, leadership must walk the talk and encourage innovation practices while making decisions.

The main purpose of business is to make money, but one can make money in many ways—legally and illegally. Thus, the purpose of a business must be clearly stated. One good definition of this purpose is "to provide value to customers by doing the right things efficiently and to make money." Customers pay for value. A business cannot make money unless the customer pays. The market capitalization of business depends upon the long-term execution of the strategy. Any short-term change in the value of the stock through short-term intent can at best be considered manipulation. Such manipulation is not the purpose of a business.

One of the leadership decisions that drives innovation in an organization is setting aggressive goals for improvement and continual change or renewal. The definition of *aggressive* can be understood as the amount or rate of change that forces one to think and do differently. For example, if one decided to make 10 percent more money at the personal level, one would think of certain incremental activities, either work more hours or earn a bonus. However, if one decided to earn 50 percent more than in previous years, one would start thinking seriously and asking questions like,

"What else can I do?" The level of change that forces us to "do differently" beyond our comfort level is labeled aggressive. Aggression is not a pie in the sky. Instead aggression means stretching current capability, resources, and thinking.

BUSINESS ASPECTS	CONVENTIONAL THINKING	INNOVATIVE THINKING
Purpose of business	Make money	Create value, and make money
Customer Demand	Satisfy	See as a larger opportunity
Leadership	Manage for quarterly profits	Lead to build a business
Decision Making	React to fix	Respond to solve systemically
Goal Setting	Easy to achieve in short term goals	Challenging long term goals
Market Analysis	Limited external knowledge	Extensive benchmarking
Direction	Random and personal	Driven by vision and values
Profitable Growth	Profit or growth	Optimized profit and growth
Organizational Values	Competitive and negative	Collaborative and positive
Employee Learning	Hire and stale skilled employees	Build and renew employee skills
Innovation	Flash of a genius	Learned skill
Improvement	Incremental	Aggressive
Method of Innovation	Brain Storming	Well defined process
Innovators	Selected few	Everyone
Resources for Innovation	Allocated sporadically	Invested continually
Building Block of Innovation	Clusters of people	Networked Individual

FIGURE 6.2 Innovation Thinking

Identifying Gaps

Launching the innovative initiative begins with an understanding of current practices. The objective is to identify strengths and weaknesses, build on strengths, and work on the areas of weakness. These steps lead to an action plan that can enable an organization to make progress. Many organizations already have similar diagnostic matrices and assessment tools. However, their adequacy is sometimes questionable because of the lack of a framework for the innovation process.

With the innovation process having been defined in earlier chapters, assessing and establishing a baseline for the elements of the innovation process in an organization is easier. Thus the assessment includes questions

Item#	Aspects of Innovation	Score (%)
1	A strategic commitment has been made to drive growth through innovation.	
2	An executive has been assigned full time to lead innovation.	
3	A strategy has been executed to accelerate innovation.	
4	Sufficient resources have been committed to support innovation activities.	
5	Departmental goals have been established to develop innovative solutions at the process level.	
6	Leadership has established a prestigious award for an innovative solution that creates exceptional value.	
7	Leadership understands the innovation process, and actively promotes risk-taking and doing things differently.	
8	A process has been established to achieve excellence in managing employee ideas.	
9	All employees have been given access to the Internet for conducting research in real time.	
10	Employees are encouraged to rotate among various departments.	
11	Company has in-house library of industry and related books and journals, and has access to on-line research services.	
12	Continual learning is rewarded at all levels, and time is allowed for learning.	
13	There is a facility for employees to brainstorm, play or experiment to test their ideas.	
14	Employees are encouraged to 'think' for new ideas for improving processes, products and services.	
15	Measures related to CEO recognition, employee ideas, and revenue from new offerings have been established.	
16	Employees are free to give funny ideas, and are not afraid of failures.	
	Average =	
Legend	0 - 20 = Ad Hoc; 21 - 40 = Marginal; 41 - 60 = Practiced; 61 – 80 = Standardized; 81 – 100 = Proven	

FIGURE 6.3 Diagnostics of Innova

about strategy, leadership, process input, process activities, process output, and measures of innovation. At the early stage, one needs to highlight critical areas for change in order to realize an innovation-friendly organization.

To evaluate each aspect of an organization, one can simply assign a percent score based on the applicable approach, deployment, and results (see figure 6.3). For example, in assessing strategic commitment for growth through innovation, one can look for clearly stated and documented objectives, its institutionalization through tactics and processes, and outcomes in terms of continual leadership interest in growth through incomes. Considering these three elements with equal significance placed on evaluating each statement, one can assign a percent score.

As for grading guidelines, one can consider a score of 0 to 20 as ad hoc, 21 to 40 as marginal, 41 to 60 as practiced sporadically, 61 to 80 as standardizing the practice, and 81 to 100 as achieving desired results. While assessing the organization's performance, one need not split hairs about the absolute score. Rather, the objective is to see the relative significance in order to initiate action to start making progress. For benchmarking purposes, the overall average can be calculated to assess future progress.

Once, a president wanted to have an initiative like "Make Money and Have Fun." Once the initiative was implemented, measuring how much money was made was easy, but measuring how much fun employees had while working in the organization was impossible. While creating a process to develop innovative ideas faster, the author realized that as people think in terms of good, crazy, stupid, and funny ideas (as described in earlier chapters), ideas became more innovative. More important, a measure of fun evolved..

Thus, one way to know when employees are having fun while working at a corporation is to measure how many funny ideas they are producing or how freely employees can present funny ideas without fear. When employees are having fun, they can pretty much say whatever they want to improve the company performance; no idea is discouraged. Being an innovative organization, you need all the funny ideas employees can come up with to improve or develop products or services.

Innovative Leadership

The success of a new strategy, without questioning its formulation, depends upon how passionately the leader champions it. Innovation has been used either as a corporate "value" or a strategy to facilitate turnaround. In either case, the CEO or executive must believe in its intended outcome; successfully drive the organization by providing direction, resources, and support; and continually engage employees through timely feedback and follow-up.

In many organizations, the leader focuses on profit and initiates cost-cutting measures, which may be necessary in the short term for a struggling company; however, in doing so, the leader acts counter to innovative thinking. Success begins with a thought in the leader's mind and is achieved through the leadership traits. Figure 6.4 organizes various leadership traits according to the process of innovation and lists the corresponding approaches of an innovation leader. People do what their leaders do, not what they ask for. Successful leaders demonstrate these behaviors and thus set an example for others to follow.

Leadership Traits	Innovative Leader
Learning	Reads a lot about a variety of subjects; interacts with community groups, employees, customers, and suppliers
Listening	Listens well to all ideas for noise, and noise for ideas
Personal style	Takes risks and executes tasks well
Interaction with employees	Encourages doing things differently better
Interaction with customers	Listens to their needs, and accepts challenges
Interaction with suppliers	Demands partnership for innovative solutions
Interaction with shareholders	Seeks support for longer term performance
Giving feedback	Rewards successes, understands failures, and encourages experiments
Behavior	Presents himself as positively enthusiastic, energetic, and an exemplary person

FIGURE 6.4 Innovative Leadership

Making an Innovation Strategy Work

Lawrence G. Hrebiniak, in his book *Making Strategy Work*, provides a template for leading effective execution and change. According to Hrebiniak and the methodology used for Six Sigma projects, one can address the following tactics for successful execution of the innovation strategy:

- Define a clear charter with cost and benefit analysis

- Identify stakeholders and utilize their influence

- Align organizational structure

- Develop a roadmap with clearly defined accountability

- Coordinate tasks and frequently share information

- Support and reinforce execution

- Manage change and culture

- Establish a process for sustaining innovation

- Reward success and inspire excellence

- Learn and adjust the strategy

A lot has been written about strategy execution; however, success depends on this ultimate factor: the desire of the leadership to make the strategy work. If a leader is committed to making innovation an integral part of doing business, it will happen. Otherwise, innovation will not occur.

Chapter Seven

Return on Innovation

Most studies show that establishing a correlation between innovation and corporate performance is challenging. Even worse, surveys of CEOs find an adverse relationship between investment in innovation and corporate performance. Such existing situations and executive perceptions may be a contributing factor to the confusion concerning the topic of innovation, as well as for the lack of commitment to systematic innovation. The best way to sustain innovation is to ensure there is a return on it.

Innovation Intent

Many companies consider growth in revenue as return on innovation; many times, growth in revenue, however, does not translate into more money for the organization—so there is no return on innovation. Though the revenue growth will somewhat reflect the role of a company's innovation, it does not say anything about the effectiveness of the innovation. To ensure a return on innovation, profit growth must also be guaranteed. Innovative products not only provide more opportunities for revenue growth, they also enable better margins on sales.

Innovation can have multiple dimensions of impact on corporate performance and can be analyzed in the following categories:

- Most innovative: revenue growth
- Best innovative: profitable growth due to innovation
- Managed innovation: a causative relationship between the investment and return
- Return on innovation: the financial return ($) on investment in innovation

The following table based on the top twenty-five innovative corporations (and a few more), according to *Businessweek*'s data for the 2003 to 2006 period shows the top five companies for the above four categories.

MOST INNOVATIVE ($ BILLION)	BEST INNOVATIVE (RATIO)	INNOVATION MANAGED (RATIO)	RETURN ON INNOVATION ($)
Wal-Mart (92)	Google	Google	Google (2.85)
GE (48)	Apple	Apple	Dell (2.83)
P&G (24)	Genentech	Dell	Apple (2.0)
Dell (20)	Amazon.com	eBay	eBay (1.74)
Motorola (20)	eBay	Genentech	Nokia (0.84)

FIGURE 7.1 Companies In Various Innovation Categories

In order for a company to sustain innovation, it must regularly introduce new products and services with significant innovation components. Such a company must also emphasize the commercialization of its innovations in order to maximize its return on innovation. As the table above shows that the return on innovation (measured in dollars) is far from being maximized. The data highlight the need for the institutionalization of innovation, as well as the improvement of both the efficiency and effectiveness of the innovation process.

Linking Innovation to Corporate Strategy

Deploying innovation with a clear mandate for expected outcomes will yield partial results. In many organizations, research and development and innovation become the end goal rather than the means by which to achieve business objectives. Innovation must create value, excitement, and return on investment through leadership, planning, and execution.

Corporations have an objective to be profitable on a quarterly basis. The challenge in managing profit by quarters leads to decisions for a quarter that require mostly action and little thought. While taking actions to cut costs, leaders often cut out innovation. Such an approach is counterproductive to creating a culture of innovation. Organizations prioritize research and development projects based on their ability to provide returns in the short term. This strategy will haunt these organizations in the long term.

Organizations must apportion resources both for long-term research on fundamental and platform innovations and for short-term development of derivative and variation innovations. Large organizations that sacrifice longer-term technological research and development in favor of shorter-term design innovations step into sudden crashes. Intel and Motorola are good examples of perennially successful companies in economic trouble because of a lack of fundamental innovations from which to develop new platform products. Intel needs fundamental innovations in process and manufacturing, while Motorola could benefit from breakthrough innovations in communication technologies.

Linking the corporate strategy to profitable growth will lead to planning for innovation at all levels. Successful companies continually look at their innovations with annual to ten- or twenty-year outlooks, in order to perpetuate the culture of innovation. Maintaining profitable growth through innovation will bring purpose to innovation activities.

Chapter Eight

Teaching Innovation

E very person is born to be creative. People do innovate for themselves, so they are not totally ignorant of the innovation process. However, most have not thought hard enough to formulate their process of innovation or creative thinking. As a result, true innovation is sporadic and rare.

Everyone knows how to walk; however, when it comes to racing, one must train intensely to compete well. Similarly, to keep up with the growing demand for providing innovative solutions and services, employees need a framework of innovation that allows them to utilize their intellectual and material resources to develop innovative solutions when needed, rather than randomly. Employees need to learn innovation using a holistic process that is easy to apply and to produce significantly innovative solutions that can generate direct or indirect economic value. The good news is that the innovation process is teachable.

Like any other human resource development initiative, organizations must establish a training program in innovation for its executives and employees. Employees directly involved in design and development must master innovation skills and achieve certain competency levels to improve the odds of their success. Employees involved in innovative improvement must also understand the framework, customer expectations (internal as well as external), and use of available resources. Two important aspects of training in innovation are creating awareness so that they can continually identify opportunities for innovation and inspiring employees to create usable, innovative solutions quickly.

Entrepreneurship is a common topic in business school curricula. However, most entrepreneurship programs lack instruction in innovation. As a result, we have many entrepreneurs who lack the ability to produce innovative solutions; hence, the survival rate of new businesses is low. Some universities offer a few courses in innovation. Due to a lack of fundamental work on innovation, however, these institutions limit teaching primarily to brainstorming and discussing past successes and failures rather than how to become innovative.

Today, more consumers are demanding customized solutions, and corporations need to respond with these custom solutions on demand. Therefore, innovation has to become a mature process, like machining processes did in the industrial age. In order for the innovation process to become a routine one, the science and engineering behind it must be developed and taught in colleges and businesses.

The Illinois Institute of Technology (IIT) has taken the lead in providing education in business innovation to its students. The following is a course I developed and have taught at IIT since 2006. After a successful run of six semesters for this course, a training and certification program was developed at IIT to teach busy executives and professionals in a shorter time frame.[2]

College Course Syllabus

Within you right now is the power to do things you never dreamed possible. This power becomes available to you just as soon as you can change your beliefs.
—Maxwell Maltz

This course is designed to teach innovative thinking through theory, methods, and practice. The course incorporates Einstein's thought processes and Edison's method to establish an innovation process that can be applied in today's business environments.

---

2   www.iit.edu/cisa.

Current economic conditions and global sourcing require that innovation become a leading tool for sharpening ones competitive edge. Innovation has so far been considered the competency only of design engineers or a select few employees; this belief is insufficient for today's reality, however. Innovation is a learned skill, and anyone can become an innovator. Corporations and organizations need innovation to develop customer-specific solutions in almost real time. Following is the typical schedule of the semester-long course:

TEXTBOOKS

Business Innovation in the 21st Century (2007) by Praveen Gupta
   Open Innovation by Henry William Chesbrough
   Making Innovation Work by Tony Davila, Marc J. Epstein, and Robert Shelton

RESEARCH ASSIGNMENT

Students write a paper or develop a presentation documenting the evolution of a new product, such as the computer, semiconductor chip, cell phone, airplane, automobile, iPod, or an item of their choice. They document key innovations and milestones to date. This assignment helps them internalize the concepts of the evolutionary nature of innovation.

SESSION	CONTENT
Week 1	Introductions, Class Expectations, Syllabus review Discussion – History of Innovation, Warm Up Exercise
Week 2	Creativity, Invention and Innovation Exercise: Understanding the Difference
Week 3	Conventional Tools of Creativity Exercise: Apply Selected Creativity Tools Guest Lecture 1
Week 4	Innovation in the Information Age & Need for Innovation on Demand/ Real Time Marketing – Discussion
Week 5	Mind Hardware and Mental Processes & Framework for Innovation
Week 6	Room for Innovation Procter and Gamble (A) – Classroom Assignment
Week 7	Innovation Project Assignment Guest Lecture 2
Week 8	Mid-Term Examination & Innovation Deployment
Week 9	Measures of Innovation & Knowing Winning Idea – Discussion Guest Lecture 3
Week 10	Innovation in Service Exercise: Identifying Measures of Innovation in Service Organization
Week 11	Protecting Innovation/ Guest Lecture 4
Week 12	Commercializing the Innovation & Innovation at 3M
Week 13	Managing Innovation, Course Review and Learning Assessment Exercise: Planning for Innovation (Research Paper & Innovation Project Due)
Week 14	Rehearsal – Project Presentations
Week 15	Project Presentations – The Student Innovator Award Competition
Week 16	Final Examination: The Innovation Project

FIGURE 8.1 A Typical Schedules Of A Semester Long Course

PAPERS / CASE STUDIES

PAPERS

Students are required to review the following *Harvard Business Review (HBR)* cases and submit single-spaced, one-page summaries to reflect their understanding. This requirement keeps their focus on understanding the customers and their requirements.

1. "Real-Time Marketing" by Regis McKenna (*HBR* 95407)

2. "Knowing a Winning Idea When You See One" by W. Chan Kim and Renee Mauborgne (*HBR* R00510)

CASES

Students should review the following cases, reflect on their understanding of the concepts learned in the class with regard to these real-life cases, and be prepared to answer a series of questions about them.

1. "Proctor and Gamble 2000 (A): The SpinBrush and Innovation at P&G" by William A. Sahlman and R. Matthew Willis (*HBR* 9-804-099)

2. "Innovation at 3M Corporation (A)" by Stephen Thomke (*HBR* 9-699-012)

PERSONAL INNOVATION PROJECT

Students apply the complete innovation methodology to an area of their own passion by identifying an opportunity and then developing an innovative solution. This project gives them an opportunity to practice the methodology using our proprietary forms. Once they are able to apply the concepts in the area of their interest, they gain the confidence to apply them in their field of work, which in most cases is not too far from their area of interest.

After they develop their innovative solution, students make a short presentation for the class, which is judged by a panel of experts who rank the top three innovations. Cash awards and certificates are big motivators for students to compete seriously for their innovation.

Training and Certification

In this age of knowledge, innovation competency is an evolving necessity at both the individual and corporate levels. By learning to be more innovative and achieving the Business Innovator Certification, people gain the confidence to innovate solutions for personal and professional growth. Given the state of the economy and the challenges faced by all people, innovation skills will enable us to create new opportunities either as entrepreneurs or as employees. In either case, we must maximize the utilization of our intellectual resources.

The Business Innovation class at IIT, Chicago, is an unparalleled course. It offers the participants a comprehensive approach to learning a reproducible methodology, from identifying an opportunity to monetizing a creative solution. After all, innovation is just applied creativity. Encouraged by exceptional feedback over six semesters of our business innovation course,[3] we have launched our innovation programs for the industry. While a semester-long course is well-suited for full-time and part-time students, busy executives want to learn quickly and start practicing innovation in a focused way. In view of their needs, the following programs have been created to further support the efforts to educate people in innovation:

1. Business Innovator Training and Certification (Innovation for Professionals)

2. The TEDOC Training (Innovation for Managers)

3. Master Business Innovator Certification (Train-the-Trainer in Innovation)

4. Innovation Overview for Executives (Innovation for Executives)

The participant must pass the Web-based Business Innovator Certification test to become a certified business innovator or a certified master business innovator.

---

3   ITM 582.

A Review of the Business Innovator Certification Test

"I just completed—and fortuitously passed—both parts of the Business Innovator Certification test. I was cautioned by Praveen Gupta, the certification program creator, that passing the test the first time through was not to be expected, and now I can clearly understand why he said that. This test isn't just a simple multiple-choice quiz, lightly touching on components of the business innovation process. It is a much more rigorous examination that builds methodically from the foundational elements of innovation—terms, definition, history—and then requires the applicant to employ a stepwise innovation-on-demand process within a ninety-minute time box that demonstrates the applicant's mastery of the discipline." — Peter Balbus, the first Certified Business Innovator, Dallas, Texas

Conclusion

The Innovation Solution equips us with a better understanding of the innovation process. In the absence of a clear understanding of this process, leadership starts the innovation initiative, commits resources, establishes measures, and then finds that innovation does not happen. However, with a deeper understanding of the process of innovation, a clearly defined strategy can be formulated and executed to achieve expected outcomes.

Like any problem, the process of innovation started out as an unsolved puzzle. This book will prepare readers to solve the innovation puzzle in their own way and enjoy the experience of being innovative.

About the Author

Praveen Gupta is the developer of the Breakthrough Innovation (Brinnovation) framework and the world's foremost authority on teaching innovation. He is the architect of the strategy for execution map, which allows corporations to increase profits in as little as nine months. He is also a recognized thought leader in the areas of excellence and innovation, an author of many books, and a champion of the intellectual engagement of all people. His management principles and methods have been implemented cost-effectively in numerous organizations ranging in size from small businesses to Fortune 50 companies.

Brinnovation is a teachable innovation framework. It is a simple but powerful approach to institutionalizing innovation in both for-profit and nonprofit organizations. His approach to innovation has led to the Business Innovator certification being offered in collaboration with the Illinois Institute of Technology, where is he is a Director of Center for Innovation Science and Applications.

Praveen was also the founding editor-in-chief of the *International Journal of Innovation Science*, which was designed to further the science and engineering of innovation. His other books include *Business Innovation in the 21st Century, The Six Sigma Performance Handbook, Stat Free Six Sigma*, and *Six Sigma Business Scorecard*, which have been translated into many languages.

Bibliography and Additional Resources

Altshuller, Genrich. *And Suddenly the Inventor Appeared: TRIZ, the Theory of Inventive Problem Solving.* Worcester: Technical Innovation Center, 1996.

Basili, Victor R. "Software Modeling and Measurements: The Goal Question Metric Paradigm." Computer Science Technical Report Series, CS-TR-2956 (UMIACS-TR-92-96). College Park, MD: University of Maryland, 1992.

Chesbrough, Henry. *Open Innovation: The New Imperative for Creating and Profiting from Technology.* Boston: Harvard Business Press, 2003.

Christensen, Clayton M., and Michael E. Raynor. *The Innovator's Solution.* Boston: HBS Press, 2003.

The Creative Problem Solving Group, Inc. "The Climate for Creativity, Innovation, and Change." www.cpsb.com.

Drucker, Peter F. *Innovation and Entrepreneurship: Practice and Principles.* NYC: Harper & Row, 1993.

———. "The Discipline of Innovation." *Harvard Business Review.* August 1985.

Gupta, Praveen. *Six Sigma Business Scorecard: A Comprehensive Corporate Performance Scorecard.* New York: McGraw-Hill Publishers, 2003.

———. "Innovation and Six Sigma, Six Sigma Columns." *Quality Digest,* December 2004. www.qualitydigest.com.

———. *The Six Sigma Performance Handbook.* New York: McGraw-Hill, 2004.

———. "Innovation: The Key to a Successful Project." *Six Sigma Forum Magazine,* August 2005.

———. "4P's Cycle of Process Management." *Quality Progress,* April 2006.

———. *Six Sigma Business Scorecard.* New York: McGraw-Hill Publishers, 2006.

————. *The Six Sigma Performance Handbook*. 2nd ed. New York: McGraw-Hill Publishers, 2006.

————. *Business Innovation in the 21st Century*. North Charleston: BookSurge, LLC, An Amazon Company, 2007.

Hrebiniak, Lawrence G. *Making Strategy Work: Leading Effective Execution and Change*. Upper Saddle River, Wharton School Publishing, 2005.

Kaplan, Robert S., and David P. Norton. *The Strategy-Focused Organization: How Balanced Scorecard Companies Thrive in the New Business Environment*. Boston, Harvard Business Press, 2000.

McCarty, Thomas, Lorraine Daniels, Michael Bremer, and Praveen Gupta. *The Six Sigma Black Belt Handbook*. McGraw-Hill Publishers, New York, 2004.

National Innovation Initiative. "Innovate America Report." National Innovation Initiative Summit and Report. 2nd Edition. Washington DC, 2005. www.Compete.org.

Neely, Andy. "In Search of a Metric System for Innovation." *Financial Times*, October 7, 2004.

Restak, Richard, MD. *Brainscapes*. New York: Hyperion, 1995.

Studt, Tim. "Measuring Innovation…Gauging Your Organization's Success." *R&D Magazine*. www.rdmag.com.

Walcott, Robert P. and Lippitz, Michael, *Grow from Within: Mastering Corporate Entrepreneurship and Innovation*. New York: McGraw-Hill Publishers, 2009.

Frequently Used or Referenced Web sites:

Accelper	www.accelper.com
Apple	www.apple.com
Business Week	www.businessweek.com
Council for Competitiveness	www.compete.org
IEEE	www.ieee-virtual-museum.org
Illinois Institute of Technology	www.iit.edu
Microsoft	www.microsoft.com
Motorola	www.motorola.com
PA Consulting Group	www.paconsulting.com
Quality Digest	www.qualitydigest.com

Quality	www.qualitymag.com
Real Innovation	www.realinnovation.com
The Creative Problem	www.cpsb.com
Solving Group	

Made in the USA
Lexington, KY
09 December 2014